THE TWO KINGDOMS

THE TWO KINGDOMS:
How You've Never Heard It Before

John Bourque

Unless otherwise indicated, all Scripture quotations are taken from the King James Version of The Holy Bible, copyright 1964, 1965, 1966, 1971 by Royal Publishers, Inc., Nashville, Tennessee. Any words in the Scripture quotations in brackets or bold letters reflect the author's own emphasis.

All Scripture quotations marked NKJV are taken from the New King James Version, copyright 1972, 1984 by Thomas Nelson Publishers, Inc., Any words in the Scripture quotations underlined reflect the author's own emphasis.

Published by Gulf Breeze Publishing.
ISBN: 978-0-9963720-0-9-8
Copyright © 2017 Gulf Breeze Publishing. All Rights reserved.

Printed in the United States of America. This book is protected by the copyright laws of the United States of America. This book may not be copied or reprinted for commercial gain or profit. The use of short quotations or occasional page copying of text for personal or group study is permitted and encouraged.

Permission will be granted upon request. The cover may not be reproduced, stored in a retrieval system, or transmitted in any form or by any means-electronic, mechanical, photocopying, recording, or otherwise in whole or in part in any form without the express written consent of the Publisher.

INDEX

FOREWORD.. 6

PREFACE 7

ACKNOWLEDGMENTS 8

IN A DIFFERENT LIGHT... 11

ACTUALLY, THEY'RE ALL MY STARS...................................... 37

AN INNOCENT MAN.. 51

SONS OF GOD... 81

THE SERPENT AND OTHER ANIMALS OF THE KINGDOMS...... 95

SALVATION PRAYER 110

FOREWORD

Several months ago, I was approached by John Bourque with a manuscript of the book you hold in your hands. His request was simple, "Read this, and let me know what you think." I must say that after I read each chapter, I wanted to know not only more about the book, but also about its author.

John Bourque is a man with a simple desire to know God better through the knowledge of His Word. Even though he graduated from Bible school long ago, he never wanted to graduate from the school of learning. He has a desire to learn God's Word without the filter of the traditions of men.

As you read this book, you will be challenged to "re-think" some of the "traditional" views you have held of God's Word. It may take some time to process some of the content of this book. That's okay. The Bible is a book that is so simple that a young person can benefit from reading it, yet so deep and multi-layered that we will be studying it throughout eternity.

One of the things that the Lord shared with John once was this statement "Some of my ministers teach what they have heard taught, not what my Word says." That statement alone will help you to understand some of the material covered.

My biggest "take away" from this book is that there is much more to the Bible than what initially meets our eye. It is my prayer that you will follow the model of the believers in Berea, in Acts 17. They took the time to study and examine the teachings of the Apostle Paul "to see if the things that they had heard were really so."

God Bless you,

Pastor Tom Arnould
Good News Church
Yukon, OK
www.goodnewschurch.tv

PREFACE

When the Lord began giving me revelation on these Scriptures in Genesis, he said, "Some of my ministers teach what they heard taught and not what my Word says." So, I endeavored to stay away from teaching on this subject and just allowed him to show me what he wanted to show me through the Scriptures.

In many cases when people have read different sections of the manuscript their response was, "This makes sense!" If you will put yourself in neutral in what you know and what you think you know, and allow the words of this book to create a picture on the inside of you, I believe you will have a more accurate picture of the beginning.

The Devil one day will be cast into the lake of fire, but until then, we're going to have to deal with him and his cohorts. I believe the Word of God through the light that the Lord gave me through his Word, when believed and applied, will help you to walk in victory over him.

The way that God and man operated in the beginning is a mirror of the way we will operate with the Lord in the future, operating through our spirits, and not through our souls.

By no means am I saying that this is the full knowledge and revelation of the total beginning. But you will see some things differently. It's important that we study God's word for ourselves. As we are walking in a more intimate, personal relationship with God the Father, Jesus, and the Holy Spirit, they are our all in all.

I challenge and encourage you to study God's Word, prayerfully study his Word. "Lord, I want to know you, how you work, why you work, how you operate. I want to know YOU!"

ACKNOWLEDGMENTS

Thank you to Josh Lease for helping me with the professional editing services. jlease@aegediting.com

A very special thanks to April Stark for painting the portrait for the cover. www.aprilstarkart.com

To D. Tucker for adding all his knowledge of the publishing process so I could have the manuscript ready to bring to publishing and distribution. www.fokuscreative.com

Susan McClarty, thank you for putting fresh eyes on the manuscript so I could get perspective.

A special thank you to Judy Williams, my friend, stylist, and sounding board, for allowing me to bounce thoughts off her and for sharing her wisdom.

To Ryan, my artistic, gifted, firstborn son, thank you for giving the visual aid, helping people to not only see in words, but in picture.

To Ashton, my youngest son, who helped with grammar and the beginning of editing, and for just living with me through all of it. It was a labor of love.

A very special thanks to my lovely, darling wife who helped put all the thoughts, ideas, and revelation altogether in one manuscript so that it would make sense to send to the editor. Without her, these words would still be in a computer. I owe her my life, blood, sweat and tears. I probably owe her something on the other side. I'll find out when we get there, but I believe there will be some eternal rewards. Plus, she's cute!

Chapter 1
In A Different Light

THE ALPHA

I would like to share with you the word, as it was revealed to me. I didn't receive this from a man or a woman, but by the revelation of the Word of God. The Lord told me that words connect peoples, places, times, and events. Now I call this, The Two Kingdoms: How You've Never Heard It Before.

Though you have no doubt read it many times before, please read through the beginning of Genesis so that the text is very fresh in your mind. Genesis 1:1-5 says,

> *"In the beginning God created the Heaven and the earth. And the earth was without form, and void; and darkness was upon the face of the deep. And the Spirit of God moved upon the face of the waters. And God said, Let there be light: and there was light. And God saw the light, that it was good: and God divided the light from the darkness. And God called the light Day, the darkness he called Night. And the evening and the morning were the first day."*

THE FIRST DAY IN THE SPIRIT REALM

What I would like to show you is that 100% of everything that happened on what the Bible calls the first day happened in the realm of the spirit, not in the natural or physical realm. Let's just imagine that God permitted you to see the beginning just like He did the prophet Jeremiah. (We will look at Jeremiah 4:23-28 shortly).

Now, if you were caught up in the Spirit and you took a picture at the beginning of the first day in Genesis where it says, "The earth was without form, and void," everything you would see took place between verse two and verse five. If you snapped another picture after verse five and then compared the two pictures, they would be identical in the natural realm.

In the spiritual realm is where all the changes took place. Everything God does, He does in the Spirit or in the spiritual realm first.

Ephesians 1:3 says,

> "Blessed be the God and Father of our Lord Jesus Christ, who hath blessed us with all spiritual blessings in heavenly places in Christ."

He has already blessed us. It is up to us, through faith, to appropriate it for ourselves.

John 4:24 says,

> "God is a Spirit: and they that worship him must worship him in spirit and in truth."

Spirit comes first, then physical.

It is very important that we allow the Bible to interpret the Bible. So, we see that in the beginning, God created Heaven and the earth—in the spiritual realm first, and then in the physical.

So remember, the Lord told me that words connect peoples, places, times, and events. When Genesis 1:1 says, *"In the beginning,"* it is actually referring to events before time. It's in what the Bible calls everlasting. Everlasting is where God created spiritual heaven and the physical earth, with everything in it. Natural gas, oil, water—He created it then. In fact, Colossians 1:16-17 says,

> "For by him were all things created, that are in heaven, and that are in earth, visible and invisible, whether they be thrones, or dominions, or principalities, or powers: all things were created by him, and for him: And he is before all things, and by him all things consist."

We know God didn't have a beginning, and He does not have an end. But some of what He created does have an end. The physical creation does have an end. The physical is temporary, but the spiritual is eternal.

Revelation 21:1-2 says,

> "And I saw a new heaven and a new earth: for the first heaven and the first earth were passed away; and there was no more sea. And I John saw the holy city, New Jerusalem, coming down from God out of heaven, prepared as a bride adorned for her husband."

God who sits on the throne is in the spiritual heaven, but the physical heaven is what He made on the second day, and the physical earth is what will be done away with at the end of time. And we who have not been hurt of the second death will experience the new heaven and the new earth. Wow! Will that be awesome!

Going back to creating heaven and earth, God is the same yesterday, today, and forever.

Malachi 3:6 says, *"For I am the Lord, I change not."*

In Genesis we read the process of the re-creation of the earth, or how He gave the earth a face-lift. You see, the very word "creation" means in its very essence to make something from nothing, and when the Word of God created the spiritual heaven, where God who sits on the throne is, He then created the physical earth. He created everything we have in the physical out of the spiritual. Everything that is in and on the earth was created then—all the water (H_2O), rock, minerals, gases and every element. He planted a garden eastward of Eden. He gave the planted vegetation in the garden the ability to grow. He formed every beast of the field. He formed man of the dust of the ground.

IN THE BEGINNING WAS IN EVERLASTING

There are some words that have more than one meaning, like "earth," for instance. Sometimes it is talking about the planet, and sometimes it's talking about dirt. You have to rightly divide to understand correctly.

This next passage, Proverbs 8:23-30, is talking about the Spirit of Wisdom. We will talk more about her later.

> *"I was set up from everlasting, from the beginning, or ever the earth was. When there were no depths, I was brought forth; when there were no fountains abounding with water. Before the mountains were settled, before the hills was I brought forth: While as yet he had not made the earth, nor the fields, nor the highest part of the dust of the world.*

> *When he prepared the heavens, I was there: when he set a compass upon the face of the depth: When he established the clouds above: when he strengthened the fountains of the deep: When he gave to the sea his decree, that the waters should not pass his commandment: when he appointed the foundations of the earth: Then I was by him, as one brought up with him: and I was daily his delight, rejoicing always before him."*

Notice the process she was referring to. All the things she talks about are physical and spiritual events in everlasting. I showed you all that to say there was a process, and a reason for the process. I believe that if God wanted to, He could have skipped the process, created, and slapped everything together at once. But He chose to use a process.

Also, and this is most important, some words have a spiritual meaning, or spiritual application, and some words have a physical meaning, or physical application. If you look at the word "death," spiritual death means spiritual separation from God who sits on the throne. Physical death is when you (your spirit and your soul) are separated from your body. We need to rightly divide what realm the scripture is referring to.

Genesis 2:17 says,

> *"For in the day that thou eatest thereof thou shalt surely die."*

Now we see that spiritually, they were separated from God who sits on the throne in heaven, and physically, Adam died about 800-plus years later.

Genesis 5:5 tells us,

> *"In all the days that Adam lived were nine hundred and thirty years: and he died."*

When Adam sinned and lost fellowship with God who sits on the throne, he was over one hundred years old. I will explain more about this later.

Notice Job 38:4-6, which says,

> "Where wast thou when I laid the foundations of the earth? declare, if thou hast understanding. Who hath laid the measures thereof, if thou knowest? or who hath stretched the line upon it? Whereupon are the foundations thereof fastened? Or who laid the corner stone thereof."

Notice the different processes in making our planet earth.

Isaiah 28:10 says,

> "For precept must be upon precept, precept upon precept; line upon line, line upon line; here a little, and there a little."

Healing is a process. Healing by definition is a recovery, progressing every day. Praise the Lord!

WITHOUT FORM AND VOID

Let's look again at Genesis 1:2:

> "And the earth was without form, and void; and darkness was upon the face of the deep. And the Spirit of God moved upon the face of the waters."

First let's look at the words "was without form and void." The Hebrew words translated 'was without form and void' are the words 'hayah tohuw bohuw'. Pronounced phonetically; [haw-yah to'-hoo bo'-hoo] The Strong's Hebrew English Lexicon and www.biblehub.com KJV Lexicon define each of the following: Hayah; a primitive root; to exist, i.e. be or become, come to pass (always emphatic, and not a mere copula or auxiliary). Tohuw; from an unused root meaning to lie waste; a desolation (of surface), i.e. desert, figuratively, a worthless thing; adverbially, in vain:-confusion, empty place, without form, nothing, (thing of) nought, vain, vanity, waste, wilderness. Bohuw; from an unused root (meaning to be empty); a vacuity, i.e. (superficially) an undistinguishable ruin:-emptiness, void.

Jesus said something that most of us understand in John 10:10:

> "The thief cometh not, but for to steal, and to kill, and to destroy; I am come that they might have life, and that they might have it more abundantly."

So we understand that if a situation is stealing, killing, or destroying, the enemy in one way or another is involved.

One thing we will see about God is that everything that He does is good, good, good, good, good, and very good! But Tohu va bohu is stealing, killing, and destroying to the (almost) highest level.

FALL OF LUCIFER

What we will see in between Genesis 1:1 and Genesis 1:2 is where Lucifer fell. Remember, words connect peoples, places, times, and events. There is only one other place in the Bible where the words "without form and void" are used together. God gave the prophet Jeremiah a divine vision of the condition of the earth after Lucifer fell. The earth was perfect, but as soon as the devil and the fallen angels were cast to the earth, it was no longer perfect.

And consequently, God's judgment fell on the earth.

Jeremiah 4:23-28 says,

> "I beheld the earth, and, lo, it was without form, and void; and the heavens, and they had no light. I beheld the mountains, and, lo, they trembled, and all the hills moved lightly. I beheld, and, lo, there was no man, and all the birds of the heavens were fled. I beheld, and, lo, the fruitful place was a wilderness, and all the cities thereof were broken down at the presence of the Lord, and by his fierce anger.
> For thus hath the Lord said, The whole land shall be desolate; yet will I not make a full end. For this shall the earth mourn, and the heavens above be black; because I have spoken it, I have purposed it, and will not repent, neither will I turn back from it."

God gave the prophet Jeremiah a picture of what the earth looked like when this event of judgment was going on.

Jeremiah saw the beginning of the judgment, whereas Genesis 1:2 was at the end of the judgment.

I want you to read two passages about Lucifer's fall so that you will have them at the forefront of your thinking as we go forward.

Isaiah 14:12-17 says,

> "How art thou fallen from heaven, O Lucifer, son of the morning! how art thou cut down to the ground, which didst weaken the nations! For thou hast said in thine heart, I will ascend into heaven, I will exalt my throne above the stars of God: I will sit also upon the mount of the congregation, in the sides of the north: I will ascend above the heights of the clouds; I will be like the most High. Yet thou shalt be brought down to hell, to the sides of the pit. They that see thee shall narrowly look upon thee, and consider thee, saying, Is this the man that made the earth to tremble, that did shake kingdoms; That made the world as a wilderness, and destroyed the cities thereof; that opened not the house of his prisoners?"

Ezekiel 28:12-19 says,

> "Son of man, take up a lamentation upon the king of Tyrus, and say unto him, Thus saith the Lord God; Thou sealest up the sum, full of wisdom, and perfect in beauty. Thou hast been in Eden the garden of God; every precious stone was thy covering, the sardius, topaz, and the diamond, the beryl, the onyx, and the jasper, the sapphire, the emerald, and the carbuncle, and gold: the workmanship of thy tabrets and of thy pipes was prepared in thee in the day that thou wast created.
>
> Thou art the anointed cherub that covereth; and I have set thee so: thou wast upon the holy mountain of God; thou hast walked up and down in the midst of the stones of fire. Thou wast perfect in thy ways from the day that thou wast created, till iniquity was found in thee. By the multitude of thy merchandise they have filled the midst of thee with violence, and thou hast sinned: therefore I will cast thee as profane out of the mountain of God: and I will destroy thee, O covering cherub, from the midst of the stones of fire. Thine heart was lifted up because of thy beauty, thou hast corrupted thy wisdom by reason of thy brightness: I will cast thee to the ground, I will lay thee before kings, that they may behold thee.

Thou hast defiled thy sanctuaries by the multitude of thine iniquities, by the iniquity of thy traffick; therefore will I bring forth a fire from the midst of thee, it shall devour thee, and I will bring thee to ashes upon the earth in the sight of all them that behold thee. All they that know thee among the people shall be astonished at thee: thou shalt be a terror, and never shalt thou be any more."

THE SIMILARITIES OF THIS EVENT

Notice the similarities in these passages, supernatural words from God, about the fall of Lucifer. These two passages connect peoples, places, times and events. The "peoples" is Lucifer and the life he messed up. Lucifer's fingerprint is stealing, killing, and destroying. So this is his fingerprint essentially. The "places" are here on earth. The "time" is when he corrupted things. The "events" would be his corruption and the aftermath of the corruption, including the deception of one-third of the angels, and the judgment from God that came after the corruption.

Isaiah 14:1 says,

"How you are cut down to the ground, You who weakened the nations." Ezekiel 28:17b, says, "I will cast thee to the ground, I will lay thee before kings, that they may behold thee."

Isaiah 14:16-17 says,

"Those who see you will gaze at you, and consider you saying; Is this the man who made the earth tremble, Who shook kingdoms, Who made the world as a wilderness, And destroyed its cities, Who did not open the house of his prisoners?"

Jeremiah 4:24 says,

"I beheld the mountains, and, lo, they trembled, and all the hills moved lightly."

Jeremiah 4:26-27 says,

> "I beheld, and, lo, the fruitful place was a wilderness, and all the cities thereof were broken down at the presence of the Lord, and by his fierce anger. For thus hath the Lord said, The whole land shall be desolate; yet will I not make a full end."

Jesus said in Luke 10:18,

> "I beheld Satan as lightning fall from heaven."

Understand something: the devil on his best day couldn't do all this destruction. When Satan fell, he was cast out of Heaven to the earth. He corrupted what was here, and God's judgment fell. And that's what we see here. After everything, God judged the earth.

THIS IS WHERE TIME BEGAN

God hid a truth in His Word, and here is how He did it. God used the same words when He was talking about the spiritual realm and the physical realm.

Then we come into Genesis 1:2,

> "And the earth was without form and void; and darkness was upon the face of the deep. And the Spirit of God moved upon the face of the waters."

Genesis 1:3 tells us,

> "And God said let there be light; and there was light."

Genesis 1:4-5 finishes,

> "And God saw the light, that it was good: and God divided the light from the darkness. And God called the light Day, and the darkness he called Night. And the evening and the morning were the first day."

What the Hebrew would hear with their ears is, God said, "light be, and light was." I have only heard this taught from the perspective of the natural, physical realm, because usually when someone reads, "Let there be light," they then say that light began to travel at six hundred and seventy million miles per hour, which is the speed of physical light.

But almost nothing could be further from the truth. Do you know the speed of spiritual light?

1 John 1:5b says,

> "that God is light, and in him is no darkness at all."

We live in this physical world, so all the words we read make pictures, but we do not have a picture for God being light. It did not say God is physical light or that God is man-made light. We know God is a Spirit, as we saw in John 4:24. The speed of spiritual light equals God IS light, God IS omnipresent.

Spiritual light is constant, and it's everywhere at once. Spiritually speaking, there is no dark side of the moon. Physically, there is a dark side of the moon, because of the line of sight from the sun. A spiritually dead spirit (the devil and his cohorts and people who are not born again) are the only locations that there is no spiritual light.

I was talking to some friends one day, and one of them said that when he gets to heaven he will travel at the speed of thought. Someone else said he will travel at warp speed. Both of them were talking as if maybe they could beat God to a place and get there before Him. Later I got to thinking: if it is a place, He's already there.

Something that we will see about what the Bible calls "the first day" is that everything that was done was done in the realm of the spirit. Also, imagine with me, if you will, darkness on the face of the deep.

If you can picture the earth without water, imagine a deep pit, or cavern, or a deep area—that is where the darkness was. And then, add the water over it.

Remember, physical water has no impact on the spirit realm. The Spirit of God moved upon the face of the waters. He was moving upon the waters, and darkness was under the water, on the face of the deep.

Romans 10:7

"Or, Who shall descend into the deep? (that is, to bring up Christ again from the dead.)"

The devil and all his cohorts were down there, in the deep.

When I was younger, I always thought when the Bible said DEEP, it was referring to the deep blue sea. What it is talking about is when Jesus went down into the deep, that's where the devil and his cohorts were. The Holy Spirit is on top of the water (see Genesis 1:2). Darkness was on the face of the deep.

If God would permit you, just like Jeremiah, to see darkness on the face of the deep, and then you take a picture of the darkness on the face of the deep at that moment, and then you go through the events of that day, and then the evening and the morning, and you take another picture, in the physical realm there would be no change, but in the spiritual realm, everything changed.

First off, there was no light. Of course, it would be dark. But that's not the darkness that the Bible is talking about. It is not referring to natural or physical darkness, but spiritual darkness or the Kingdom of Darkness. It was Satan and his cohorts. They were the ones that were on the face of the deep.

Understand that the spiritual realm is not influenced or affected by physical light or physical darkness, physical heat or physical cold. Not one bit.

THE KINGDOM

Now, watch this: when God said, "Light, be," since God is light, He simply said, "Me who is light, be," or, "Me, be." God invited Himself back into the earth (I'll explain more on this and give you an illustration shortly).

When He came into the earth, He saw it was good. He divided the light from the darkness, or the Kingdom of Light, over which domain He is King, from the Kingdom of Darkness.

Let me ask you this: Who is the light of the world?

John 8:12 says,

> "Then spake Jesus again unto them, saying, I am the light of the world: he that followeth me shall not walk in darkness, but shall have the light of life."

This is when He became the light of the world. He is light, and was always light. But when God came into the world, that's when He became the light of the world.

The Apostle Paul understood what happened here.

In 1 Thessalonians 5:5 it says,

> "Ye are all the children of light, and the children of the day: we are not of the night, nor of darkness."

Later, 1 Thessalonians 5:8a says,

> "But let us, who are of the day, be sober."

He is talking about the Kingdom of Light, which God called "day." He was not talking about physical day, physical light or darkness.

Now we have a picture of this. The next time there is an altar call and someone comes forward to receive Jesus as his Lord and Savior, when he comes to the altar he is in darkness, living in the Kingdom of Darkness. Then, he gets born again.

On the outside, everything is the way it was—his hair is the same, clothes are the same, shoes are the same. But on the inside, he is a new creature in Christ. Old things pass away; and, behold, all things become new. Once God moves in, He begins working on the natural.

When I was at Bible school we would sing a song: "I got the Holy Ghost on the inside working on the outside, oh what a change in my life." God comes in spiritually, then He works on the natural, molding it into His image.

So, in the same way, God invited Himself into the world and began to work His perfect plan and purpose in everything.

When we invite, or receive Him, in our lives, He comes in us to make His abode in us. He begins working His plan and purpose for our life as we allow Him.

SEPARATION PERIOD

Genesis 1:5 says,

> "And the evening and the morning were the first day."

The evening is the period that separates the light, or day, from darkness, or night. Morning is the period that separates the darkness, or night, from the day, or light. But again, these are spiritual terms.

In Revelation 2:28 we read,

> "I will give him the morning star."

Also, in Revelation 22:16b, Jesus said,

> "I am the root and the offspring of David, and the bright and morning star."

These are all spiritual terms: morning, light, darkness.

Because we live in this natural world, we gravitate naturally in our thought process. Let us go to Daniel chapter eight.

You will need to read the whole chapter, but Daniel 8:26 says,

> *"And the vision of the evening and the morning which was told is true: wherefore shut thou up the vision; for it shall be for many days."*

So do you see it is not talking about the natural morning, because of the sun and the rotation of the earth?

I'm going to show you when, where, and why we started thinking like this. Remember, everything God did on the first day, He did it in the spirit—100%.

GOD IS WHO THEY ARE

Before we go any farther, we must gain some understanding. There is God the Father, God the Son, and God the Holy Spirit. One God. They are God. They are their names. We call them the Trinity—Father, Son, and Holy Spirit. God is who they are; God is who He is. When you talk about God, you are talking about God the Father or God the Son or God the Holy Spirit.

Allow me to take this down a couple of levels. I knew a man. His name was Bill Board. He had two sons, Clip, and Switch. If I told you that I talked to Mr. Board yesterday, you don't know which Mr. Board. Was it Mr. Switch Board or Mr. Bill Board, or maybe, Mr. Clip Board? You don't know. Perhaps it is Bill Board's brother, Black Board, who has a daughter, Peg. But, unless I tell you the first name, you will not know.

With God, it's the same thing. Is it God the Father, God the Son, or God the Holy Spirit? Sometimes to identify, you need to know their ways, or their jobs. For instance, God the Father didn't die on the cross. He sent His Son (John 3:16). In the beginning, it was the same way.

Hebrews 11:3 says,

> *"Through faith we understand that the worlds were framed by the Word of God, so that things which are seen were not made of things which do appear."*

A lot of times we say that God spoke this world into existence, and He did. Without question, He spoke this world into existence. But this scripture is not talking about what most preachers preach.

I have a question for you: John 1:1-3 says,

> "In the beginning was the Word, the Word was with God, and the Word was God. The same was in the beginning with God. All things were made by him; and without him was not anything made that was made."

My question for you is: Who is the Word? Yes, he's Jesus. Sometimes we look at words as pictures or capsules, which make images in our minds. But **THE WORD WAS MADE FLESH** and dwelled among us (John 1:14).

When you see the Word of God, remember, that's His name. He is the Word of God. He was the Word of God. And He will forever be the Word of God.

Revelation 19:13 says,

> "And he was clothed with a vesture dipped in blood: and his name is called The Word of God."

Names had meaning when the Bible was written. You are your name; your name is you.

When God, who sits on the throne, named the Word, at that moment, all the power of God, as well as all the love of God, was at work. All the grace, faith, life, wisdom, and knowledge of God went into the naming of God, whom we call the Son of God.

Whenever there is a name change, it is for a purpose and reason. God has many names, or name changes.

For instance, God the Father in the New Testament is known as God our Abba Father.

Romans 8:15 says,

> "For you did not receive the spirit of bondage again to fear, but you received the Spirit of adoption by whom we cry out, 'Abba, Father.'"

He wasn't Abba Father in the Old Testament.

In John 14:16-17 we read,

> "And I will pray the Father, and He shall give you another Comforter, that he may abide with you for ever. Even the spirit of truth; whom the world cannot receive, because it seeth him not, neither knoweth him: but ye know him; for he dwelleth with you, and shall be in you."

So back to John 1:3:

> "All things were made by him: and without him was not anything made that was made."

Talking about Jesus, Colossians 1:16 says,

> "For by him were all things created, that are in heaven, and that are in earth, visible and invisible, whether they be thrones, or dominions, or principalities, or powers: all things were created by him, and for him."

So if it was created or made, visible or invisible, it was created or made by God, the Word of God. We will see this all play out in Genesis. Let's back up to Genesis 1:1 for greater understanding.

I now want to inject a word so you will know who it is talking about in Genesis 1:1 when it says,

> "In the beginning God [the Word] created the heaven and the earth."

Remember, if it was created or made, it was by the Word of God, or the person who is the Word of God.

Skip down to Genesis 1:3 where we read,

> "And God [who sits on the throne] said, Let there be light: and there was light."

Remember, God who sits on the throne spoke this world into existence. God who sits on the throne did the speaking, and the Word of God did the creating, and making, and the re-entering into the earth.

With this understanding, let's go on to take a new look at the rest of this passage from Genesis.

Genesis 1:4-15 says,

> "And God [the Word] saw the light, that it was good: God [the Word] divided the light from the darkness. And God [the Word] called the light Day, and the darkness he called Night.
> And the evening and the morning were the first day. And God [who sits on the throne] said, let there be a firmament in the midst of the waters, and let it divide the waters from the waters. And God [the Word] made a firmament, and divided the waters which were under the firmament from the waters which were above the firmament: and it was so. And God [the Word] called the firmament Heaven. And the evening and the morning were the second day. And God [who sits on the throne] said, let the waters under Heaven be gathered together unto one place, and let the dry land appear. And it was so.
>
> And God [the Word] called the dry land earth; and the gathering together of the waters called he Seas: and God [the Word] saw that it was good. And God [who sits on the throne] said, Let the earth bring forth grass, the herb yielding seed, and the fruit tree yielding fruit after **his kind**, whose seed is in itself, upon the earth: and it was so. And the earth brought forth grass, and herb yielding seed after **his kind**, and the tree yielding fruit, whose seed was in itself, after **his kind:** and God [the Word] saw that it was good. And the evening and the morning were the third day.
>
> And God [who sits on the throne] said, Let there be lights in the firmament of the heaven to divide the day from the night and let them be for signs, and for seasons, and for days, and years: And let them be for lights in the firmament of the heaven to give light upon the earth: and it was so."

At this point, God who sits on the throne, by saying what He said by His Spirit, gave the Word of God all the physics, distance, speed, and geometry for our solar system. He used wisdom, knowledge, understanding, discretion, and discernment, because He is all that.

Hebrews 1:3 says,
"And upholding all things by the word of his power."

Because of who He is—He is God—He is all power. And who did we say His Word was? The Word of God. Now He, the Word of God, could begin being a doer of the word that was spoken.

We pick back up with Genesis 1:16:

> "And God [the Word] made two great lights: the greater light to rule the day, and the lesser light to rule the night: he made the stars also. And God [the Word] set them in the firmament of the heaven to give light upon the earth. And to rule over the day and over the night, and to divide the light from the darkness: and God [the Word] saw that it was good. And the evening and the morning were the fourth day. "

He made them the exact size, putting them at the precise distance and at just the right angle. He set it all in motion, and at the right speed—even the earth's orbit and the rotation.

Because of that we have physical day and night, signs and seasons, and days and years. Now I do not know how old the earth is, but according to the Bible, the sun, the moon, and the stars, were all created and made on the fourth day.

ANIMALS AND CREATURES

Genesis 1:20-21 tells us,

> "And God [who sits on the throne] said Let the waters bring forth abundantly the moving creature that hath life, and fowl that may fly above the earth in the open firmament of heaven. And God [the Word] created great whales, and every living creature that moveth, which the waters brought forth abundantly, after their kind, and every winged fowl after **his kind**: and God [the Word] saw it was good."

One thing I believe the Scripture is bringing out right here, is that some, not all, of the vegetation and animals were to be created and made after **his kind**, implying a replication of what He has already created and made.

Jeremiah 4:25 says,

> "I beheld, and lo, there was no man, and all the birds of the heavens were fled."

This indicates that before the first physical judgment, the birds were in heaven operating fine. Did you notice "*all the birds of the heavens were fled,*" not just half of them, or most of them?

Now God who sits on the throne wanted them on earth. In verse 21 of Genesis 1, it says "*after their kind,*" which means they will produce after themselves. But when it says after **his kind**, that implies past tense ownership. Create these like the ones you have or have created prior to this.

In heaven, they are not known as animals but "creatures." We know what the image of the creatures look like in heaven because of what Adam called them here on earth ("*And whatever he called them, that was their name,*" Genesis 2:19.)

John said in Revelation 4:7,

> "And the first beast was like a lion, and the second beast like a calf, the third beast had the face of a man, and the fourth beast was like a flying eagle."

Prophets and apostles have mentioned seeing visions of oxen, different colored horses, and even the Tree of Life.

There is the Tree of Life in the Garden of Eden and in heaven (the word is plural, so there is more than one tree. The Tree of Life is probably a species of tree. See Revelation 2:7 and Revelation 22:2).

In fact, in Revelation 19:11 it says,

> "And I saw heaven opened, and behold a white horse; and he that sat upon him was called faithful and true."

Notice the horse was in a male gender.

I believe that heaven and earth mirror each other. I believe they looked more identical before the fall of Lucifer (see Isaiah 12:19), the judgment of God (see Genesis 1:2,9), God's curse on the ground (see Genesis 3:17-18), and Noah's flood (see Genesis 6:17).

All of these changed how closely heaven and earth mirrored each other. They are not identical to each other, but there are overwhelming similarities.

In Revelation 22:1, notice a river of water in heaven. We have rivers of water on earth. The tree of life is on either side of the river in heaven (see Revelation 22:2). The earth has the tree of life in the Garden of Eden. God is on the throne. The earth has thrones. There are different books in heaven. We have books. Revelation 4:5 refers to lightning and thunder. We have lightning and thunder on the earth.

Of course there are also living creatures in heaven that look like our animals here on earth. One difference, according to the Bible, is the creatures of heaven can't procreate. The procreating is for the life that is on this planet earth. Heaven has streets, so does the earth.

Heaven has every precious stone, so does the earth. Heaven has windows; we have windows. In heaven, the windows will be open to you when you tithe and give offerings here on earth. Isaiah 14:13-14 says, *"in heaven there are the Stars of God, upon the mount, the north, and the heights of the clouds."* The stars of God are the angels of God; we have the angels of God working for us, and ministering to us, and we have natural stars. We have north direction, and mounts, and clouds.

Heaven has gates; we have gates. In the book of Revelation it mentions doors in heaven, a rainbow, and palms in their hands. We have doors, rainbows, and palms in our hands, too. Heaven has a sea; we have seas. Heaven has incense; we have incense. The Word of God is everything about the beginning, and everything about the ending.

Revelation 1:8 says,

> *"I am Alpha and Omega, the beginning and the ending, saith the Lord, which is, and which was, and which is to come, the Almighty."*

In this earth we have the law of physics, but in heaven it is the law of faith.

Because we are spirits, when we use the law of faith, that causes heaven to supersede the law of physics, and allows the supernatural to have reign in our life.

Remember, it can be the same word, but spiritually and physically they may be different. In fact, in Revelation 10:3-4 we read seven thunders had uttered their voices. So the thunders are heavenly creatures.

Our spirit bodies and our natural bodies mirror each other. Our spiritual ears hear the voice of God, and our natural ears hear natural voices. In our spirit, we discern His Word, and with our intellect we reason natural things. Also, we gain revelation in our spirits and illumination in our minds.

That's why God gave us a brain, which is a natural organ and which is the dwelling place of our soul, our mind and intellect, our emotions, and our will. God's original intent was that man would operate in the spirit, totally loyal to the Word of God who is a Spirit, and living life as God knows it and lives it. (We will talk more about this later.)

HIS KIND, IN HIS IMAGE

Genesis 1:22-23 says,

> "And God blessed them, saying, Be fruitful, and multiply, and fill the waters in the seas, and let fowl multiply in the earth. And the evening and the morning were the fifth day."

Genesis 1:24 goes on to say,

> "And God [who sits on the throne] said, Let the earth bring forth the living creature after **his kind**, cattle, and the creeping thing, and beast of the earth after **his kind**: and it was so. And God [the Word] made the beast of the earth after **his kind**, and cattle after their kind, and everything that creepeth upon the earth after **his kind**: and God [the Word] saw that it was good."

So God created animals after their kind.

But what about mankind?

Genesis 1:26 reads,

> "And God [who sits on the throne] said, Let us make man in our image, after our likeness: and let them have dominion over the fish of the sea, and over the fowl of the air, and over the cattle, and over all the earth, and over every creeping thing that creepeth upon the earth. So God [the Word] created man in his own image, in the image of God [who sits on the throne] created he him: male and female created he [the Word] them."

Man was created and made spiritually. You are a spirit, and you have a spiritual body. You have a soul. The Word of God formed a physical body out of the dust of the ground to be our spirit and soul's dwelling place, our earthly tabernacle. God has a soul also, but He, unlike us, is not led by it.

Let's read 2 Peter 3:9,

> "The Lord is not slack concerning his promise, as some men count slackness; but is longsuffering to us-ward, not willing that any should perish, but that all should come to repentance."

Suppose God granted you a divine appointment in heaven right now. You would go up—your inner man, the real you. Your spirit man would experience the appointment, and when you got back to your body, then you could think about the divine appointment. Your physical body, or your earthly tabernacle - that's yours for the earth, not for heaven. When you leave this world, your natural physical body will stay and take on decay, or it may be burned up. But that's alright because you won't need it anymore. You will be in a spiritual place, and you are a spirit and have a spiritual body.

GOD SPEAKING TO MAN AND BEAST

God is about to speak to man and beast, which He just created, and bless them.

We read in Genesis 1:28-31:

> "And God [the Word] said unto them, be fruitful, and multiply, and replenish the earth, and subdue it: and have dominion over the fish of the sea, over the fowl of the air, over every living thing that moveth upon the earth. And God [the Word] said, Behold, I have given you every herb bearing seed, which is upon the face of all the earth, and every tree, in the which is fruit of a tree yielding seed: to you it shall be for meat. And to every beast of the earth, and to every fowl of the air, and to every thing that creepeth upon the earth, wherein there is life, I have given every green herb for meat: and it was so. And God [the Word] saw everything that he had made, and, behold, it was very good. And the evening and the morning were the sixth day."

Remember in John 1:3 it tells us, *"All things were made by him: and without him was not anything made that was made."*

After the work of creation, God rested.

Genesis 2:2-3 tells us,

> "And on the seventh day God [the Word] ended his work which he had made; and he rested on the seventh day from all his work which he had made. And God [who sits on the throne] blessed the seventh day, and sanctified it: because that in it he had rested from all his work which God [the Word] created and made."

GENERATIONS

In Genesis 2:4 we read,

> "These are the generations of the heavens and the earth when they were created, in the day that the Lord God made the earth and the heavens."

When it says, "These are the generations," it is referring to heaven and earth before time existed. It was a spiritual heaven (where God is sitting on His throne), the heavenly host, and a physical planet, called earth.

Another generation was when He created time, came back to the earth and called the light Day (who He is).

God made the earth and the heavens, a firmament that divided the waters from the waters.

So generations of the earth are two periods—an everlasting period and a timed period, when he called the light Day. Each generation indicates a period: one was a period before time, which the Bible calls everlasting. And one was a period of time, when He made time as we know it. Genesis 2:4 is referring to both events.

Revelation 1:8 tells us,

> "I am Alpha and Omega, the beginning and the ending, saith the Lord, which is, and which was, and which is to come, the Almighty."

Everything about the beginning is the Word of God.

Revelation 19:13 describes the Word by telling us,

> "And he was clothed with a vesture dipped in blood: and his name is called The Word of God."

Chapter 2
Actually, They're All My Stars

This chapter is what the Lord showed me about the word star in the Bible. I would like to share it with you. First of all, like most of the study of this book, we will look at how words have more than one meaning—spiritual, physical, and sometimes a metaphor. Jesus often spoke in metaphors or parables. The dictionary defines metaphor:

1. A figure of speech in which a term or phrase is applied to something to which it is not literally applicable in order to suggest a resemblance, as in *"A mighty fortress is our God."*

2. Something used, or regarded as being used, to represent something else; emblem; symbol.

The word star has four main uses in the Word of God. In Genesis 1:16 we read that God created the sun, moon, and stars. In this instance, the word stars is talking about the literal stars that we see in the nighttime sky. Also, we can easily see four planets, which appear brighter than the stars. Usually they are the first star look-alikes we see at dusk, and at dawn they are the last star look-alikes we see. But they aren't stars; they just reflect light. Real stars are the source of their own light.

There are a few times when star is used in a metaphor representing something else in the Bible.

For instance, in Genesis 37:9 we read,

> *"And he dreamed yet another dream, and told it his brethren, and said, Behold, I have dreamed a dream more; and behold, the sun and the moon and the eleven stars made obeisance to me."*

Joseph's eleven brothers didn't like that dream. God used the eleven stars in this dream to represent his eleven brothers. This revealed to him something about the future.

The name Lucifer literally means "daystar." We know he is a created being, and he was and is an angel.

This is found in Ezekiel 28:14-15, which we read earlier.

> "Thou art the anointed cherub that covereth; and I have set thee so: thou wast upon the holy mountain of God; thou hast walked up and down in the midst of the stones of fire. Thou wast perfect in thy ways from the day that thou wast created, till iniquity was found in thee."

Day is referring to light, and it is and was a spiritual term.

Genesis 1:5 says,

> "And God called the light Day, and the darkness he called night…"

Remember, angels are spirits. They were all created to do God's work and minister to us who shall be heirs of salvation. So Lucifer was created an angel of light, or an angel of God.

We've seen that the light on what the Bible calls the first day was spiritual, and that God called that spiritual light Day. Who is the light of the world? His name is the Word of God, Jesus.

John 8:12 says,

> "Then spake Jesus again unto them, saying, I am the light of the world: he that followeth me shall not walk in darkness, but shall have the light of life."

He said He was the light of the world, and He called light Day. Remember, 1 Thessalonians 5:5 says,

> "Ye are all the children of light, and the children of the day: we are not of the night, nor of darkness."

This light and darkness is not physical, but spiritual.

Let's continue with more spiritual metaphors for the word star.

In Judges 5:20 we read,

> "They fought from heaven; the stars in their courses fought against Sisera."

When you see something that is out of the ordinary, the Bible is often not speaking literally—it is speaking in a metaphor or spiritually. The stars here are angels.

Job 38:7 says,

> "When the morning stars sang together, and all the sons of God shouted for joy."

This would have taken place after man was created and before the flood of Noah. The term morning refers to a period coming out of darkness, into His marvelous light: A new Day and a new light. It was referring to the angels who didn't leave their first estate, and to the sons of God who are the children born of Adam, before they sinned. The inhabitants of the earth, the sons of God, had different times when they came together to reverence and worship God. And the heavenly host (the angels), must have joined in with them, at least from heaven's perspective (I am not sure if mankind knew it or not).

You may remember from Isaiah 14:13 that it says, *"For thou hast said in thine heart"*—notice he didn't say it with his mouth but in his heart—*"I will ascend into heaven, I will exalt my throne above the stars of God: I will sit also upon the mount of the congregation, in the sides of the north."* The "stars of God" are the angels of God. Lucifer wanted to be above all of God's angels.

Daniel 8:10 says,

> "And it waxed great, even to the host of heaven; and it cast down some of the host of the stars to the ground, and stamped upon them."

Stars are referring to angels. Some were cast out of heaven to the earth. It was God who cast Lucifer out, but it was because of his sin that he was cast out. The other angels that he was able to deceive were cast out with him.

STARS IN THE NEW TESTAMENT

Revelation 1:16, 20 says,

> "And he had in his right hand seven stars... The mystery of the seven stars which thou sawest in my right hand, and the seven golden candlesticks. The seven stars are the angels of the seven churches: and the seven candlesticks which thou sawest are the seven churches."

The seven stars are the seven angels.

Revelation 8:10-11 tells us,

> "And the third angel sounded, and there fell a great star from heaven, burning as it were a lamp, and it fell upon the third part of the rivers, and upon the fountains of water; And the name of the star is called Wormwood: and the third part of the waters became wormwood; and many men died of the waters, because they were made bitter."

Revelation 9:1 goes on to say,

> "And the fifth angel sounded, and I saw a star fall from heaven unto the earth: and to him was given the key of the bottomless pit."

"To him" is in the male gender, referring to the star that John, the writer, saw. To him was given a key to the bottomless pit. The word star is again referring to an angel.

Revelation 12:4 tells us that the devil and the angels that he deceived got cast to the earth:

> "And his tail drew the third part of the stars of heaven, and did cast them to the earth: and the dragon stood before the woman which was ready to be delivered, for to devour her child as soon as it was born."

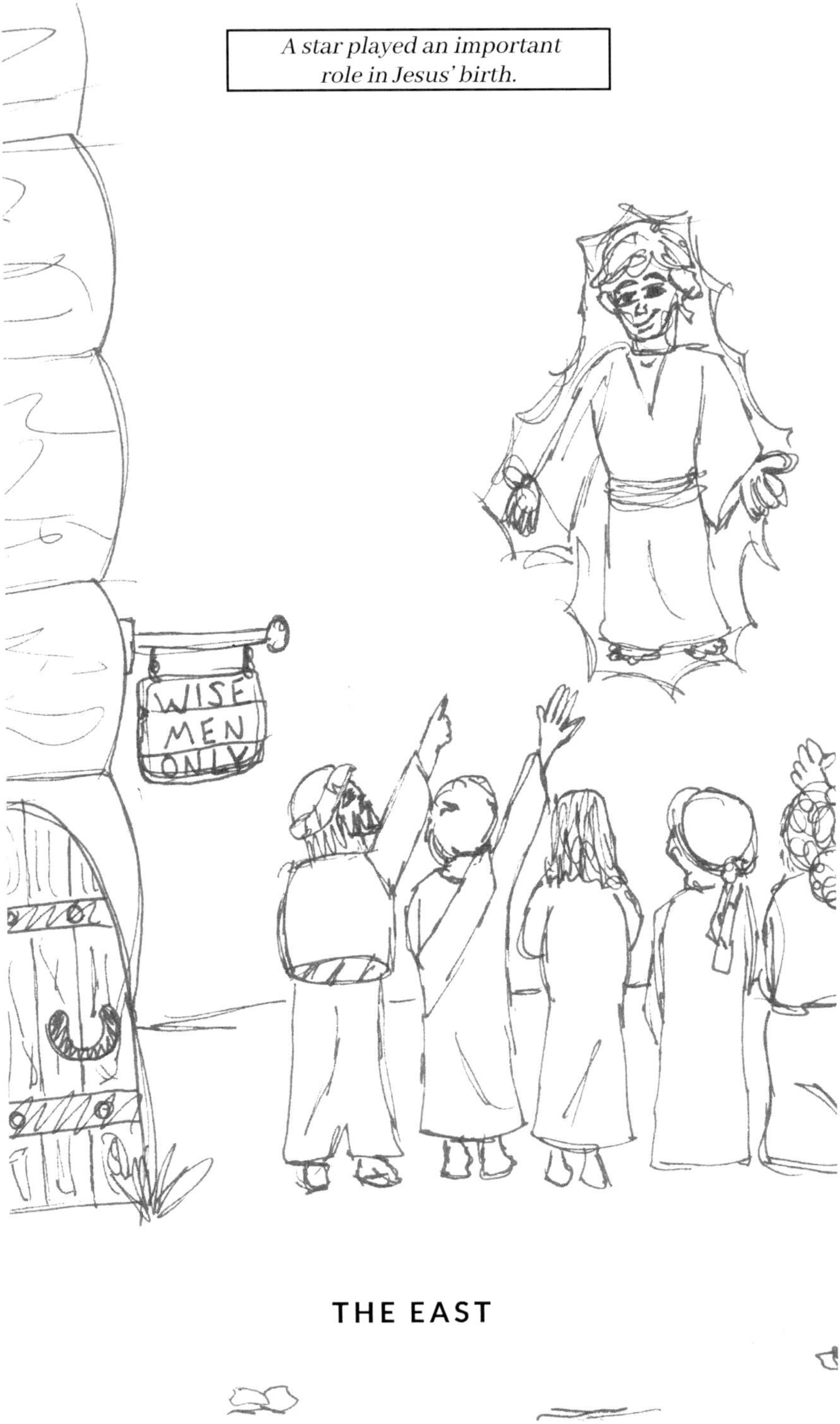
A star played an important role in Jesus' birth.
WISE MEN ONLY
THE EAST

Matthew 2:2 reads,

"Saying, Where is he that is born King of the Jews? For we have seen his star in the east, and are come to worship him."

When I read this, all of a sudden, a voice inside said, "That star was an angel." I thought that statement was different than what I had been taught. In fact, a church I used to go to sold a book in their book store that was supposedly a hard read. It made claim to have identified the star which led the wise men to Bethlehem, in the land of Judea. Also, on Christmas cards you sometimes see a bright and twinkling star high in the sky. So, at first, it didn't make sense to my head.

I said, "Lord, you're going to have to show me in your Word in a place or two that proves that statement, or I won't believe it." The Word says, "So that in the mouth of two or three witnesses every word shall be established." I was reading from the New King James version, and the voice inside said, "Notice the wording."

Matthew 2:9 says,

> "When they had heard the king, they departed; and, lo, the star, which they saw in the east, went before them, till it came and **stood** over where the young child was."

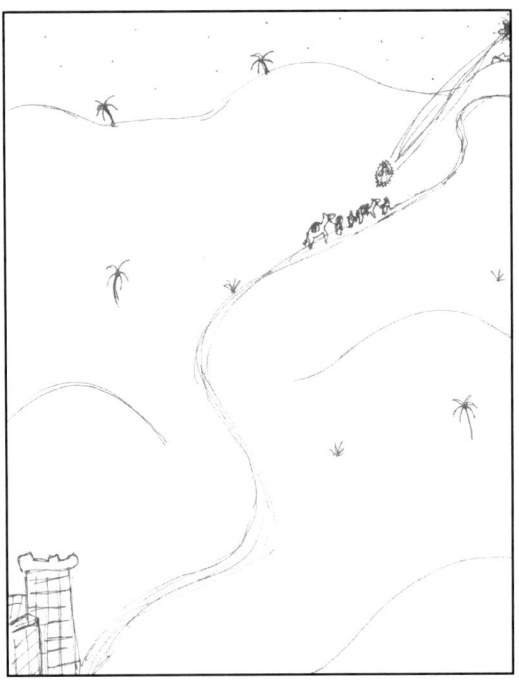

Actually, They're All My Stars

The star **stood** over where the young child was.

Think about this: Scientists say that our sun is one of the smallest stars in our universe, and our sun is approximately one million times the size of the earth. A natural star would be big beyond big, and very hot.

But an angel...?

In Luke we will look at, or around, the birth of Jesus and note what the angel did.

Luke 2:9 says,

"And behold, an angel of the Lord **stood** before them, and the glory of the Lord shone around them, and they were greatly afraid."

Did you notice the angel **stood** before them, and the star **stood** over where the young child was?

A star is a metaphor for angel, as sometimes we have seen in the Word of God.

Also, we could probably name that star. He would be the angel of the Lord.

Another note: the wise men were, in their day, educated above most. When they use certain words and terms, sometimes it is above us, like doctors of our day. If a doctor tells you, "You have dermatitis," and you ask, "What's that?" he will say, "It is a skin disease." The wise men would have been highly educated in the scriptures, and God told them about his Christ. They got the honor and privilege of worshiping Him as a young child.

When I was a boy, our family put a star and sometimes an angel on top of our Christmas tree. And after the Lord showed me all this, I thought, "Does everyone know this but me?" But I found out that most people don't know. That's why this side journey was important. Something good to ponder!

A DRIVE IN NORTHEAST OKLAHOMA

One day in December, I was driving my truck in northeast Oklahoma. I was kind of tired, so I turned the radio on to teaching. I wasn't getting good reception, and a minister was speaking. He said, "You know I think the Lord's star was a planet, because they are brighter than all the other stars." But when he made that statement he didn't have a witness of the spirit. He knew that the statement was incorrect, so he tried to salvage the statement and said, "Well, in any case it was the Lord's star." And right after he said that, the voice inside said, "Actually, they're all my stars."

I thought about it for a few seconds. God created them, and made them, and He put them where they are today. I said, "Lord, you're right, they are all your stars."

Then I lost the reception on the radio. I sure enjoy when the Lord speaks into my life, even when it is correction.

Everything about God is to help us to gain and keep a more intimate relationship with him that we may experience as close to heaven on earth as possible. I bless and praise His holy name. God is so good, and his mercy endures forever!

WANDERING STARS

The word planet comes from the Greek planetes meaning "wanderer," from planaein "to wander." The planets look like wandering stars.

In Jude 1:6 we read,

> *"And the angels which kept not their first estate, but left their own habitation, he has reserved in everlasting chains under darkness unto the judgment of the great day."*

Jude 1:13 goes on to say,

> *"Raging waves of the sea, foaming out their own shame; **wandering stars**, to whom is reserved the blackness of darkness for ever."*

If you look at a planet in the sky every night, you will notice it moves a little each night. Stars are fixed in their place, appearing to move seasonally as the earth orbits the sun. But planets look like wandering stars.

Angels of light are fixed stars, metaphorically speaking. The angels that kept not their first estate are wandering stars.

They look like stars of light, but they wandered out of their course—or what God intended for their plan and purpose, to do and to be.

Our natural stars and planets are a physical picture, not a duplication, of a spiritual reality. Just like we see physical light and physical darkness, spiritual light and spiritual darkness; In the same way, we have a physical man and a spiritual man.

We have physical eyes and ears and spiritual eyes and ears. We even have physical taste and spiritual taste. We have physical touch and spiritual touch. Smell is also physical and spiritual.

We have five physical senses and five spiritual senses. God illuminates our mind and gives revelation to our spirit: That is spirit-to-mind and spirit-to-spirit. Two different realms have two different laws. The physical realm has physical laws. The spiritual realm has spiritual laws. The physical law is to go get something naturally. The law of the spirit is to operate by faith with the word of faith (see Romans 10:8-10).

Chapter 3
An Innocent Man

The devil and his cohorts, as powerful as they are, have no power over you unless you give it to them.

Genesis 4:6-7 gives us the first account of the enemy's activity after the fall of man:

> "And the Lord said unto Cain, Why art thou wroth? And why is thy countenance fallen? If thou doest well, shalt thou not be accepted? And if thou doest not well, sin lieth at the door. And unto thee shall be his desire, and thou shalt rule over him."

What we are seeing here is that Cain didn't do well in his offering to the Lord, but the Lord said if he did well, he would be accepted. So it was in Cain's power and ability to do well; he just didn't.

What we are going to study here is the behind-the-scenes activity of the enemy, and how we give him place in our lives—or not.

Cain got very upset, and even after verbal correction and instruction from the Lord, he didn't change. We always have a choice to make a constructive response or a destructive response. In fact, no response, we will see, is a destructive response.

Jesus said in John 8:44,

> "You are of your father the Devil, and the desires of your father you want to do. He was a murderer from the beginning, and does not stand in the truth, because there is no truth in him. When he speaks a lie, he speaks from his own resources, for he is a liar and the father of it."

Jesus called the devil a thief and a liar. John 10:10 says,

> "The thief cometh not, but for to steal, and to kill, and to destroy: I am come that they might have life, and that they might have it more abundantly."

When God uses names, it has the most accurate meaning possible and helps paint the most accurate picture possible.

So through his lying and deception, the devil tries to steal, kill, and destroy.

An Innocent Man

I believe the more we understand the full meaning of some of the Bible's words, the greater the picture and the understanding we will have. What we will see is that some of the devil's cohorts are mentioned in a male gender.

Take for instance sin. I was taught that when we do something wrong, according to the Bible, it is sin—and it is. But allow me to introduce him to you, because you deal with him every day. Read Genesis 4:7 again:

> "And if thou does not well, sin lieth at the door. And unto thee shall be **his** desire, and thou shalt rule over **him**."

Familiar spirits have an assignment to certain individuals to help influence and motivate them through imagination and thought and circumstances in the kingdom where they have domain—the kingdom of darkness. Everything about that kingdom is death or leads to death.

First of all, spiritual death is when a person is spiritually separated from God who sits on the throne. Physical death is when your spirit and your soul are separated from your earthly tabernacle, or your body.

Then there is the spirit of Death and his best friend, Hell. They work closely together.

Revelation 6:8 we read,

> "And I looked, and behold a pale horse: and his name that sat on him was Death, and Hell followed with him."

Revelation 20:13-14 tells us,

> "And the sea gave up the dead which were in it; and death and hell delivered up the dead which were in them: and they were judged every man according to their works. And Death and Hell were cast into the lake of fire. This is the second death."

First Corinthians 15:26 says,

> "The last enemy that shall be destroyed is death."

So every time you read the word death in your Bible, you need to rightly divide which death it is referring to. Remember, at the beginning names were more significant and very accurate in their meaning. Death is who he is, and all he can do; apart from death he can do nothing. It is the very fiber of his being. In fact, Jesus experienced first spiritual death and then physical death, on our behalf.

SPIRITUAL DEATH

Matthew 27:46 reads,

> *"And about the ninth hour Jesus cried with a loud voice, saying, E'lī, E'lī, lāma sa-bach'-tha-ni? that is to say, My God, my God, why hast thou forsaken me?"*

God who sits on the throne looked down on His Son as the offering for the sin of the world. Remember, *"Christ hath redeemed us from the curse of the law, being made a curse for us: for it is written, Cursed is every one that hangeth on a tree:"* Galatians 3:13

Jesus' relationship with God the Father was severed, His eyes were opened, and He spiritually lost fellowship with God.

I say this with tears—we can't even come close to comprehending what Jesus experienced. He is the Word of God—He who is God and who didn't have a beginning—and, in fact, He never knew being without God who sits on the throne, never ever. This was the first time He was out of contact with God who sits on the throne, and it was because of us, and for us, that He tasted death, once and for all, as our substitute. This was the spiritual redemption.

Remember, Adam was told by the Word of God that if they ate of the tree they would surely die (see Genesis 2:17).

They died first spiritually, separated from a spiritual, functioning relationship with God who sits on the throne.

It was like a spiritual umbilical cord with God, who sits on the throne, was cut off.

For Adam, the supernatural being created without sin, operating in the spirit, was natural.

Genesis 3:7 tells us,

> "And the eyes of both of them were opened, and they knew that they were naked."

Now they began operating in a lower state of being—their five physical senses ruling them and guiding them. So they were operating only on what they had and what they possessed. They had to acquire knowledge with their five physical senses. Now they had to process everything through their intellect. So they went from a perfect relationship and source to imperfection, death and lack—and, to some degree, they were on their own.

Genesis 5:5 says,

> "And all the days that Adam lived were nine hundred and thirty years: and he died."

Adam died first spiritually, and then he died physically later. They were spirits, but they lost their spiritual access to what was normal before the fall. They had lived by faith, and there was no other way to live—until they ate of the tree from which God commanded them not to eat.

PHYSICAL DEATH

Jesus died physically; His Spirit was separated from His physical body. In Luke 23:46 we read,

> "And when Jesus had cried with a loud voice, he said, Father, into thy hands I commend my spirit: and having said thus, he gave up the ghost."

Jesus paid the price for sin; it was a price that we couldn't pay.

First of all, He lived a sinless life all the way through his last breath. Second, He was totally obedient to God who sits on the throne. Philippians 2:8 tells us,

> *"And being found in fashion as a man, he humbled himself, and became obedient unto death, even the death of the cross."*

So He didn't sin or miss God before He was anointed with the Holy Ghost or after He was anointed with the Holy Ghost.

Jesus was fully man, and there are certain sins like lying, stealing, or gossiping that He could have committed—but He didn't! No, not even once!

There are also spiritual sins that He had the opportunity to commit, such as not flowing with the Spirit or not doing or not saying something according to the Spirit's leading. But in these, too, He remained blameless.

It was not Jesus' will, but God's will be done. Jesus modeled selflessness, and He was totally submitted to God who sits on the throne. Jesus was faithful and worthy. He didn't sin.

So when Jesus went to hell, it was the place of departed spirits. You should read Luke 16:19-31 for an accurate picture of hell before Jesus arose from the dead.

Back then, hell was divided into two parts, one part was a place of torments, with a great gulf fixed between: and the other part He called "paradise" (see Luke 23:43).

When Lazarus the beggar went to paradise, Father Abraham comforted him. He was no longer experiencing fear, worries, anxieties, or anything the enemy could offer from the kingdom of darkness. So there was peace and tranquility that he would have never known until then.

Jesus went to the paradise side of the place of departed spirits, not the torments side.

If you read Luke 16:19-31, you see the place of departed spirits is spiritually in the physical earth in a like manner to the way you (your spirit) is in your physical body.

Read 1 Samuel 28:7-16. Notice as you read this passage, five different times it mentions to bring someone up from the dead. God permitted Samuel to go back up from the dead and speak to Saul. He came up from paradise, also called Abraham's bosom. In fact, when Samuel came up, he wasn't a familiar spirit and the woman cried with a loud voice. She wasn't used to seeing a real human spirit, just familiar spirits. So the place of the departed spirits was divided into two areas. One area is called torments, or Hell, and the other is called paradise, or Abraham's Bosom. Do not forget, the fallen angel named Hell only has rule and reign in this one area. So because it is his domain, it is called after him "Hell." He is the spirit assigned and in control of this fiery prison, where people and angels are awaiting their final destination, the lake of fire.

There is a great gulf fixed between the fires of hell and paradise, or Abraham's Bosom. Abraham's Bosom is the place where the departed spirits that are in covenant with God went. Ephesians 4:8-10 states,

> *"Wherefore he saith, When he ascended up on high, he led captivity captive, and gave gifts unto men. Now that he ascended, what is it but that he also descended first into the lower parts of the earth? He that descended is the same also that ascended up far above all heavens, that he might fill all things."*

After Jesus poured out His blood in the heavenly holy of holies, and His sacrifice was fully accepted, then He moved paradise up to heaven. When Jesus was raised, the people of paradise were raised also. Remember the Apostle Paul in 2 Corinthians 12:4 and how he was "caught up" into paradise. So paradise is now up in heaven, and now that is where the children of God go when their spirit and soul depart from their earthly body.

Now, here is some of the behind-the-scenes that we sometimes miss.

In 1 Corinthians 2:7-8 we read,

> "But we speak the wisdom of God in a mystery, even the hidden wisdom, which God ordained before the world unto our glory: Which none of the princes of this world knew: for had they known it, they would not have crucified the Lord of glory."

When we observe in the natural, we see that the Roman government, persuaded by the Jewish leaders, had Jesus crucified. But from a spiritual or behind-the-scenes look, it was the princes of this world.

Did you ever wonder how Jesus arose from the dead with the keys of hell and of death? In Revelation 1:18 Jesus says,

> "I am he that liveth, and was dead; and, behold, I am alive for evermore, Amen; and have the keys of hell and of death."

When Jesus went to hell, He didn't cross the great gulf fixed between paradise and torments and beat the devil up to get the keys.

Romans 3:23 says,

> "For all have sinned, and come short of the glory of God."

Romans 6:23 tells us,

> "For the wages of sin is death; but the gift of God is eternal life through Jesus Christ our Lord."

Ever since the fall of Adam, there have always been two groups of people on the earth. In fact, before Jesus was raised from the dead *"and led captivity captive, and gave gifts unto men,"* (Ephesians 4:8) there were two groups of people and two compartments in hell: the sons of God and the sons of men.

There are the sons of God—children of promise, covenant people, also people who lived and had not reached the age of accountability, and they were all in paradise.

These are people who are in covenant with God, who sits on the throne, the children of light and children of the day.

The second group were the sons of men—the children of darkness and of the night, people who were not in covenant with God—and they were in torments. Allow me to shed some light on this.

Jesus is the sinless Lamb of God. What happened was the devil killed Jesus; he killed an innocent man. The wages for sin is death, but Jesus never sinned. So it was unlawful that He should die. So the devil was judged. John 16:11 says, *"Of judgment, because the prince of this world is judged."*

The judgment? Guilty!

If you want another picture of this behind-the-scenes event, I refer to Brother Kenneth E. Hagin's testimony from when he died and went to hell. He said he leaped out of his body and began to descend down, down, down. He looked back up at the face of the earth, and the light of the earth grew dim until it was gone and he was in total and utter darkness. He finally reached the bottom of the pit, and as though he were being sucked there, he began moving toward the gates of hell. Isaiah 14:9 says,

> *"Hell from beneath is moved for thee at thy coming: it stirreth up the dead for thee."*

A creature named "Hell" was moving to meet him at his coming. But all he could look at was the fire through the gates. The creature grabbed him by the arm to escort him in. Brother Hagin said he knew that if he went through the gates of hell, that there wouldn't be any turning back—that he would be there forever.

And as they were approaching the gates, all of a sudden, God spoke.

Brother Hagin said he didn't understand what was said, because it was not spoken in the English language, and he was unsure of how many words were spoken. It could have been six words or twelve words. But when the words were spoken, the whole place shook, and the creature let go of his arm. And like a suction he began moving backward to the edge of the bottom of the pit, and then began moving up through the thick darkness, toward the face of the earth.

I refer to this event because God who sits on the throne judged the devil because he killed Jesus, an innocent man.

He spoke out the judgment, and all of hell and heaven would have known it.

Colossians 2:14-15 tells us,

"Blotting out the handwriting of ordinances that was against us, which was contrary to us, and took it out of the way, nailing it to his cross; And having spoiled principalities and powers, he made a shew of them openly, triumphing over them in it."

Man, don't you think the devil and all his cohorts were furious when Jesus and all the people in paradise went up to heaven and they saw them no more? They had never had control over them, but at least they were there.

The devil was now stripped of all the controlling power and authority that he gained at the fall of man!

Adam sinned, or committed high treason, and turned over his place of authority to the devil. But then the devil sinned and was stripped of all the control and authority that he gained through the fall of Adam.

Jesus legally gained back all the authority!

Romans 5:16-19 says,

"And not as it was by one that sinned, so is the gift: for the judgment was by one to condemnation, but the free gift is of many offences unto justification. For if by one man's offence death reigned by one; much more they which receive abundance of grace and of the gift of righteousness shall reign in life by one, Jesus Christ. Therefore as by the offence of one judgment came upon all men to condemnation; even so by the righteousness of one the free gift came upon all men unto justification of life. For as by one man's disobedience many were made sinners, so by the obedience of one shall many be made righteous."

God didn't deceive the devil; he just let him be who he is. He is a liar. He steals. He kills. He destroys.

Remember in 1 Corinthians 2:8, it says,

> "Which none of the princes of this world knew: for had they known it, they would not have crucified the Lord of glory."

Jesus asked the Father to forgive the men that crucified Him, for they didn't know what they were doing.

The spirits, princes of this world, were the ones responsible, influencing the men to commit this action.

JOB

I want to show you another example; it's in the book of Job. In Job 1:11 we read,

> "Satan said to the Lord, But put forth thine hand now, and touch all that he hath, and he will curse thee to thy face."

The devil has access in the thought realm, imagination, and intellect, and that is where we reason. When we reason based on our five physical senses, in our mind it can seem right. But what may seem right in the natural realm isn't necessarily correct or truth.

God always calls those things which be not as though they were, at least when it pertains to the fallen state of His creation (see Romans 4:17). That is the supernatural creative way to exist—not calling those things that are as though they are, or those things that are as though they're not. It's calling those things that be not as though they were.

The enemy puts thoughts in our thought realm; we give them action or voice, and that determines the outcome. Satan said Job would curse God to His face.

Notice the words of Job's wife: "*Then said his wife unto him, Dost thou still retain thine integrity? Curse God, and die*" (Job 2:9).

I like what Brother Hagin would say about us entertaining the thoughts the enemy sends our way: "You can't keep birds from flying over your head, but you can keep them from making a nest in your hair."

The enemy injects thoughts that seem reasonable to our five physical senses. Satan's cohort was giving imaginations or thoughts to Job's wife. She didn't rebuke them or cast them down but instead spoke them out. That's why God's Word must be our final authority.

It's up to us to police our response to all thoughts, imaginations, and words that we speak.

HOW THE DEVIL OPERATES & HOW YOU CAN COUNTER HIS ATTACKS

Proverbs 18:21 tells us,

> "*Death and life are in the power of the tongue: and they that love it shall eat the fruit thereof.*"

What you speak forth gives the unseen realm the right to act or not act, whether it is the kingdom of light or the kingdom of darkness.

That's why when we speak God's Word or keep Him in remembrance of His Word, that enables the kingdom of light to bring itself to pass in our lives.

Remember John 8:44b:

> "*When he speaks a lie, he speaks from his own resources, for he is a liar and the Father of it.*"

When we speak what we know using our five physical senses, it doesn't mean we are speaking the truth.

God's Word is truth. His Word created, empowered, enabled, directed; it loves, gives life, and *"is living and powerful, and sharper than any two-edged sword, piercing even to the division of the soul and spirit, and of the joints and marrow, and is a discerner of the thoughts and intents of the heart"* (Hebrews 4:12).

If you don't know God's Word, you don't know truth; you only know in part.

THE ENEMY TRIES TO GAIN GROUND

I would like to show you three different areas the enemy tries to gain access in every believer's life. First, when the enemy speaks to the believer, he uses thoughts and imaginations. He only has access in the realm of the soul, and he will always give you thoughts according to your vocabulary. For instance, if something scared you, you wouldn't think, "It gave me a fright" if that is not part of your vocabulary. He uses your imaginations and thoughts to get you to agree with and act on them and then speak them forth. Then he can bind you with chains of fear or pride, self righteousness, lust, being a busy body, or being judgmental. (And, don't forget, you only know in part, so that makes you a poor judge.)

The enemy speaks to you in the areas that are your weak points; things you have been redeemed from; or areas where the enemy is trying to gain some ground to speak to you.

When you have a thought about something contrary to the Word of God, that thought did not originate with you. It originated from the enemy.

All believers have areas in their lives that they have to pay more attention to. It could be addictions, coveting, worrying, unforgiveness—the list goes on. For example, if you struggle with unforgiveness and you have a simple little thought about the event that you are holding against someone, it may put you in disgust.

Suddenly you are hashing it all out again and maybe thinking of how you can get even. Or if that person got hurt, you might think to yourself, "Well, it would serve them right," or, "Maybe I could just hit them up side the head with a baseball bat—then I would feel better. At least I'd get a little vengeance."

That thought is contrary to the Word of God.

But Romans 12:19 says,

> *"For it is written, Vengeance is mine; says the Lord, I will repay, saith the Lord,"*

Thoughts or pictures that you get about a problem area in your life will enable the thoughts to persist or not—depending on what you do with them. You can actually dislike people and not want to be around them and yet be giving them a big place in your life—because you have not forgiven them. Because you haven't forgiven, you may find that when you think of them and what they did to you, you may get depressed or isolate yourself or act hatefully. But all you have to do is forgive them!

Depending on the situation, sometimes you need to walk it out a little bit. If need be, a lot—it may not be a quick process. Yet love never fails. When you wholeheartedly pray for those who have hurt you, believing God for His best in their lives, it really closes the door for the enemy to have an inroad in this situation, in your life, and in their lives. You know when you are walking in forgiveness when your thoughts and intentions towards that person are pure and holy.

Or you may have a problem with alcohol. You may already have a conviction against you for driving under the influence of alcohol. You're at work, and you hear someone there telling one of their stories about the weekend. It may have involved alcohol, and your imagination might be, "What would have changed if I were there? For sure one more case of beer." After all, you would have been thirsty, and there's no sense stopping with three beers—you're not some little kid, you can handle it, right?

At different times that day, you might be thinking of past alcohol experiences—good or bad—and maybe some future plans. Your thoughts may go to your D.U.I. and the excuses for why or how it happened. And all the time thoughts and imaginations about the taste and the feeling you get, especially when it's hot outside and the beer is cold. Man, how refreshing! You may like it so much that it doesn't matter if it's hot or cold outside, or if the beer is hot or cold—you think, "Just give me another beer, thank you!"

People sometimes feel better about themselves when their minds are affected by alcohol. This is a false, deceptive feeling. People will say or do things they normally wouldn't say or do.

So all these thoughts came from one overheard conversation. Then with your imagination you entertained these thoughts all day.

Have you ever been somewhere special, and you had a bizarre, immoral, or out-and-out nasty thought and you wondered, "Where did that come from?" You might have even said out loud, "Where did that come from?" The enemy has access in the soulish realm, but you are the final authority of what you do and what you say.

In 2 Corinthians 10:3-6 we read,

> *"For though we walk in the flesh, we do not war after the flesh; For the weapons of our warfare are not carnal, but mighty through God to the pulling down of strongholds; Casting down imaginations, and every high thing that exalteth itself against the knowledge of God, and bringing into captivity every thought to the obedience of Christ."*

You are the understood subject here—you are to pull down the strongholds and uproot them from your life and domain.

You are to cast down imaginations and every high thing that exalts itself against the knowledge of God. And you are to take every thought captive to the obedience of Christ.

Remember, if you have a thought and you answer the thought, the thought didn't originate with you, whether you agree or disagree with the thought. God speaks to your spirit, and the enemy speaks to your thought processes.

If you don't look or listen carefully, you will think these thoughts are from you. Every thought or imagination that the enemy gives you is deceptive and attempts to steal, kill, and destroy. That's all it can do. You have to keep your guard up so you don't fall prey to his devices.

LUST OF THE FLESH

If lust of the flesh is one of the areas you need to particularly pay more attention to, and you hear someone talking as they are walking up beside you, you may have a thought, "Wow, their voice sounds hot!" Then the thought of how they sound motivates you to turn to see them. Now your second thought about the person is, "Yeah, wow! Man, oh, man, they look like poetry in motion. That person is perfect. They look like a tall glass of sweet tea!" Remember, even though you answer the thought, the thought did not originate with you. It is up to you to control your thoughts according to the written Word of God.

Just a side note, thank God for beautiful and handsome people, but it is up to us to keep our desires in check or under control. I thank God for motorcycles—as long as I keep them in their proper place and they don't rule me. It isn't right if I'm looking at all that chrome and listening to the sound of the engine rumbling through the exhaust pipe, and my heart is beating profusely, and I'm drooling all over myself. It's important that we don't let our fleshly desires rule us. Let's get them in check and enjoy the bike.

Thank God for nice homes, as long as you own your home and your home doesn't "own" you. Your self-worth is not in what you own or what you have. All those things are temporary. Your self-worth should be in who you are in Christ, as sons and daughters of God. That is eternal.

You know what your weak areas are. When you listen, it may be a slight imagination, a picture or a thought, a feeling or a wonder or question in your head, or your thought process—if it's out of line with the Bible, it could be from the enemy. If those thoughts have your heart rate racing, they can affect your physical and spiritual well-being.

You can also have thoughts about getting sick and worry, "I hope I don't get the flu; you know it's flu season." The different commercials are saying "it's going to be bad this year," and you let those thoughts fester. Then maybe you're working around the house, maybe stretching a little more or different than usual, and the next morning when you get out of bed your back is sore or your legs hurt. And suddenly your mind snaps back to that thought about the flu. The thought is going along with what you feel, so you think it must be right.

Sometimes our thoughts are based on what or how we feel. You may sneeze or cough and think, "I hope I'm not coming down with something." Just a simple thought based on your five physical senses—and sometimes not based on anything at all. But will you give it place or not? You may feel pain in one of the joints of your body, and a thought comes, "Arthritis!" Maybe it runs in your family.

Well, even if arthritis runs in your family, praise God, the last generation was the last generation that will be affected if you will walk in your redemption through Jesus and what He did in His life, death, burial, and resurrection!

I have had my body hurting and all these thoughts about what was wrong going through my head about this disease and that disease. But I didn't need the devil telling me that—I could feel it strongly in my body.

And then a thought would come that so-and-so died from this disease, and man, oh man... Right there, I have the decision to make: will I entertain this? Absolutely not! I refuse that and I rebuke that! Isaiah 53:5 says,

> "But he was wounded for our transgressions, he was bruised for our iniquities; the chastisement of our peace was upon him; and with his stripes we are healed."

Not only am I healed, but with those same stripes I shall remain healed. To God be all the glory!

God's Word is the final authority in our lives. As we believe it, receive it, and confess it, then no matter what we're experiencing, His power and ability is unleashed in our lives and will bring itself to pass. It is important that we understand who we are and what we have in the redemptive work of Christ at Calvary. We need to know what we are redeemed from and what we are redeemed unto. The only way to know that is by reading, believing, and receiving the written Word of God, the Holy Bible. As God gives illumination to your mind and revelation to your spirit, you will begin to operate in the redemptive work of Christ. You will never operate above your revelation of God's Word. You may experience it once in awhile, but you won't operate in it.

But, praise God, as you pray and spend time in the Word of God, you will begin to get more illumination in your mind and revelation in your spirit, and you will begin to operate in that light.

Suicide—any thought you may have about suicide comes straight from the enemy. He might inject these thoughts or thoughts similar to these: "This family would be better off without you." Maybe you got hurt by a certain person, and you don't want to be hurt anymore ever again. Maybe this person hurt you, and you think you can't live like this anymore.

Maybe you think of the relief you will have not having any more problems. Perhaps you feel that everywhere you turn it's just another pain, just another problem. Some ask, "Why can't you just have had a normal life?" Others have a thought about the future and it looks bleak at best and they think, "Why live any longer? No one will miss me." They may feel like, "This world would probably be a better place without you here."

Notice how some of these thoughts talked directly to you. But they came in from the outside. It is sometimes easier to recognize a thought that comes straight from the enemy when he uses words like "you" in the thought.

The Bible calls the devil the accuser of the brethren. He is accusing you night and day. You may have a thought about how tired you are of all this, and then say, "Yes, I am so tired and frustrated with dealing with everything." Remember, whether you agree or disagree with the thought, that thought did not originate with you.

One way the devil tries to deceive us is by injecting thoughts according to circumstances from all the different pains of the heart, let downs, and the shattered dreams of life.

Maybe someone died or cheated on you, or it seems like everyone and everything is against you. Perhaps even your dog doesn't act happy to see you lately.

Your thoughts come from your mental faculties, but will you allow what's going on around you to dictate your future? You may hear a good report about what someone did or received. If the enemy is trying to suppress you, and if you listen to him, you may have a thought, "That will surely never happen to you." Or, "They are just lucky; you're not."

When you experience a situation that is contrary to the Word of God, it is important to find the answer to your problem in the Bible. God's Words are Spirit and they are life. And God's Word has all the creative power of God when mixed with faith in love to change any situation.

Mark 9:23 says,

> "Jesus said unto him, If thou canst believe, all things are possible to him that believeth."

I would like to make sure we are clear: Not every thought we have comes from the devil. In fact, he gets blamed for thoughts and stuff he didn't do. That's the way we shift blame from ourselves, so we can feel better about ourselves. Again, every believer has different areas in their lives that they have to pay more attention to. And with that, some people are more negative, insecure, prone to gossip or worry, have low self-esteem, or struggle with fear. The list goes on and on.

Stay aware of the areas that you are weak. When a thought or an imagination that doesn't line up with the Word of God rolls through your mind, answer it with the Word of God.

THROWING YOU OFF YOUR PURPOSE

When thoughts try to derail you from your purpose or from God's purposes for your life, they are not from Him. For instance, you make a decision you are going to have a special quiet time with God, so you begin to pray. "Man, I am so in love with you Father, God! I will bless the Lord at all times. His praises shall continually be in my mouth..."

Then you have a thought: "The laundry."

You push that thought to the side, because you have purposed to have time with God. "It's me and you, God. Father, you are so absolutely good, and your mercy endures forever..."

Then another thought comes: "I could just put a load in real quick." You answer the thought, "Yes, but I have plenty of time to do that later." Resuming your time with God, you pray, "Lord Jesus, thank you for paying the price for our sin. Thank you for loving me when I was unlovable."

The thought comes: "Socks! Yes all of them are dirty. Well, I could start the load of laundry and continue on with my quiet time..."

Now watch out for a mess somewhere or if you are hungry. You think, "Maybe just a small bowl of ice cream. I wonder if I have any chocolate chips, and maybe a little drizzle of chocolate syrup? I wonder if I have some whipped cream?"

And watch out if someone calls you on the telephone. Two hours later, you're getting really hungry because it's close to mealtime, you haven't done the laundry—you kind of forgot when you got distracted by the ice cream—and your quiet time fell short of your intent.

It turned into "ice cream snack time while chatting on the phone" time.

"Well there's always tomorrow, Father—just me and you."

Thoughts can come that try to get you off task.

You may begin to feel some symptoms, and you are more ready to succumb to them because in your thought process that's all you've been hearing or thinking. Every thought we have must be examined in light of the Word of God to make sure it is in line with what God says.

If you plead the blood of Jesus over you and your family and you thank God for the protective hedge of the blood, and then you have a thought that is contrary to the protective hedge of the blood, it is your job to rebuke the thought and replace it with what the Word of God says in that particular circumstance. You need to apply the Word of God by speaking forth the truth that applies to the wrong thought.

Just a side note, isolation is one of the enemy's greatest tools in keeping people bound up, in their own thoughts and in their own worlds, away from everyone else. Thoughts may come that make you think no one would understand what you are going through, that you are the only one in your situation. The enemy will try to keep you isolated, making you feel that you are a burden to others. Or you might feel that they might understand some of your situation, but not all of it, so you keep to yourself. The devil can also keep a person bound by telling them that what they are going through is too shameful, too embarrassing to be shared. Everything the devil communicates to you is a lie. He wants to keep you bound, keep you isolated. So seek counsel or help in whatever you are walking through.

We see in James 5:16,

> "Confess your faults one to another, and pray one for another, that ye may be healed. The effectual fervent prayer of a righteous man availeth much."

THE ENEMY COMES TO STEAL THE WORD

Something that is tightly interwoven with this is how the devil tries to steal the Word from our hearts. Jesus is talking about believers and disciples and is explaining the meaning of the parable of the sower in Mark 4:3-32.

He's talking about five different ways the enemy tries to steal the word. Mark 4:13-19 says,

> "And he said unto them, Know ye not this parable? and how then will ye know all parables? The sower soweth the word. And these are they by the way side, where the word is sown; but when they have heard, Satan cometh immediately, and taketh away the word that was sown in their hearts. And these are they likewise which are sown on stony ground; who, when they have heard the word, immediately receive it with gladness; And have no root in themselves, and so endure but for a time: afterward, when affliction or persecution ariseth for the word's sake, immediately they are offended. And these are they which are sown among thorns; such as hear the word, And the cares of this world, and the deceitfulness of riches, and the lusts of other things entering in, choke the word, and it becometh unfruitful."

The enemy is out to influence everything he can in order to remove the effectiveness of God's Word from our lives. The more of the Word of God he can steal, the less spiritual faith and power and ability we have in our lives.

God's Word is His will. If the devil can keep the effectiveness of God's Word from our lives, we will never fulfill God's will and we will never operate in all of the power of God.

The devil's goal is for the sons of God to only live as the sons of men, so that everyone lives on equal terms under his domain. So he used affliction, persecution, the cares of this world, the deceitfulness of riches, and the lust of other things to make the Word of God to have no effect or place in our life. We are spirits, but we live in a natural world, and the devil uses the natural, soulish situations to try to keep us on his turf.

But I have good news, because no matter where you are in the parable Jesus referred to, you can mature and grow up spiritually as you desire and walk in a more intimate relationship with God. Also, you will then be able to worship the Father in spirit and in truth more intimately, because that is what the Father seeks.

Mark 4:20 tells us,

> "And these are they which are sown on good ground; such as hear the word, and receive it, and bring forth fruit, some thirtyfold, some sixty, and some an hundred."

TITHING AND THE BLESSING

I have never heard of the devil tempting or suggesting to someone to tithe. If you do not tithe and you have a thought, "Should I tithe?" or, "I should begin tithing" it doesn't come from the enemy! Does it line up with the Word?

Leviticus 27:30 says,

> "And all the tithe of the land, whether of the seed of the land or of the fruit of the tree, is the Lord's. It is holy to the Lord."

So the tithe is His, and it's holy to Him. I believe one reason it is holy to Him is because of the window of opportunity it opens up for Him, and the window of opportunity it opens up for His children.

Malachi 3:8-11 says,

> "Will a man rob God? Yet ye have robbed me. But ye say, Wherein have we robbed thee? In tithes and offerings. Ye are cursed with a curse: for ye have robbed me, even this whole nation. Bring ye all the tithes into the storehouse, that there may be meat in mine house, and prove me now herewith, saith the Lord of host, if I will not open you the windows of heaven, and pour you out a blessing, that there shall not be room enough to receive it. And I will rebuke the devourer for your sakes, and he shall not destroy the fruits of your ground; neither shall your vine cast her fruit before the time in the field, saith the Lord of hosts."

I was always taught that ten percent of what I earned is called the tithe—a tenth part of—and that I was to give it to my local church, the storehouse. If I didn't do that, then I was robbing God. If that is what you were taught, allow me to show you the other side of the coin, if you will. See Malachi chapter three is showing man to God—shall a man rob God? I would like to show you God to man.

I think sometimes when we give our tithes and offerings in the church service, after the service we walk out to our car and maybe walk around our car looking for a bag of cash or something to see if God blessed us or not. Now, God is not against you finding a bag of cash, but that's not God's best. I would like to show you the number one way God blesses His people. It's found in Genesis 1:22 and 1:28. I believe if we set our sights on the right target we are more likely to hit the target and receive from God.

God is the God of relationship, and He communicates with His people. In verse twenty-two God is talking to animals, but the principles are the same:

Genesis 1:22 says,

> "And God blessed them, saying, Be fruitful, and multiply, fill the waters in the seas, and let fowl multiply in the earth."

Genesis 1:28 says,

> "Then God blessed them, and God said unto them, Be fruitful, and multiply, and replenish the earth, and subdue it: and have dominion over the fish of the sea, and over the fowl of the air, and over every living thing that moveth upon the earth."

I like to call Malachi chapter three "the open flow of words." He's opening the windows of heaven to us—that's the open—and pouring out—that's the flow—a blessing that we don't even have room enough to receive.

It comes through His Word. That's the open flow of words.

See, when you get the Word of God, you get the plan of God. When you get the Word of God, you get the purpose of God. When you get the Word of God, you get the will of God. Because God's Word is His will. When you get the Word of God, you get God.

We need to understand something about God: that God is a giver. In fact, "*God so loved the world, that he gave his only begotten son*" (John 3:16).

But in James 4:8 it says,

> "*Draw nigh to God, and he will draw nigh to you.*"

Now, the understood subject is you. You draw nigh to God, and He will draw nigh to you. You make the first move, then He makes the second move.

In Malachi 3:7 about half-way through the verse, God is speaking and He says,

> "*Return unto me, and I will return unto you.*"

Again, the understood subject is you.

You return to Me, and I will return to you. You return to God, and He will return to you.

So, in actuality, the way we rob God is when we don't give our tithes and offerings, then we rob God of the opportunity to give us the open flow of words from heaven! We also rob Him from being able to rebuke the devourer for our sake. If we don't make the first action, He can't make the second action.

Remember, God is subject and bound to His Word. So if you are not operating with the open flow of words from heaven, and the devourer isn't rebuked for your sake, then I don't care what you have in your possession or what your portfolio looks like, you are cursed with a curse, according to Malachi 3:9. God doesn't want you cursed, so He made a way for you to be blessed in His Word.

But it is up to us to do our part—not just giving our tithe but giving in faith and believing that God will perform what He said in His Word.

Side note: God is expecting us to tithe and give offerings as He wills. It's up to us to be obedient to His Word. Here in the United States, we pay taxes—federal and state taxes. Some people send money in quarterly, and some people have money taken out of their paychecks. But we all pay our taxes. If you don't pay your taxes, you could be put in prison.

With all due respect, if you are not tithing and giving offerings in faith, you are in a spiritual prison, isolated and bound, and you're not experiencing the open flow of words from heaven. Also, the enemy will have greater access in your life.

I believe we copy God. My spiritual "mom-in-the-faith" owned a restaurant that was a well-known franchise. The person who owned the franchise received a certain percentage of the money made at her restaurant. That is the agreement of the franchise and owner. She had to prepare everything according to franchise specification. They had already figured out what works, and it was her job to comply by their rules and procedures in order to continue using the franchise name. In our society we understand ownership, pink slips, and title deeds.

Check this out: God created everything. He created minerals in the ground, oil, water, precious stones, all vegetation, air, and animals. He made some things that reproduce after themselves. He created man in His image and after His likeness. God created and communicated with man, who is a spirit, on the sixth day. Then, after their bodies were formed out of the dust of the ground, they were on the earth, which God created. So God is the Creator and maker of all.

In fact, we don't even own ourselves. In 1 Corinthians 6:20 we see, *"For ye are bought with a price: therefore glorify God in your body, and in your spirit, which are God's."* He owns it all. He made it all. It's all His. He knows how it works, and He knows what is good for it.

So no matter what industry we're in, it's all God's. You may deal with animals as a veterinarian, a rancher, a butcher, a taxidermist, or leather-worker—it's all God's. You may deal with what comes from the ground—gold, salt, diamond, water, coal, dirt, whatever—

everything on this earth and in this earth, plus the air and all the gases in our atmosphere, anything taken from the moon, and even the leftover of a meteorite, is all created by God. It is all His.

He is just so gracious to allow us to use it while we are here! He wants His franchise fee, so to speak, and the amount is summed up in three words: tithes and offerings. And we get the profit of what He gives us to steward!

When we do it His way, Heaven's windows are opened, God is speaking to us, and the enemy is rebuked for our sakes. The only thing better than this is living in Heaven itself.

RECAPPING

Not every thought you have comes from the devil, but if the thought doesn't line up with the Word of God, it is your responsibility not to give it place in your life. So whether it was from the enemy or you, it doesn't matter: cast it down so it has no place in you.

Philippians 4:8 tells us what we should think on:

> "Finally, brethren, whatsoever things are true, whatsoever things are honest, whatsoever things are just, whatsoever things are pure, whatsoever things are lovely, whatsoever things are of good report; if there be any virtue, and if there be any praise, think on these things."

If you keep your mind on these things, then you will experience more peace and will begin to think like God.

I would like to show you the negative side of this if you don't mind. When people are yielding to sin, it gives the enemy an inroad into their lives. I am not talking about demon possession but actually oppression. Let's look at pride—when people are prideful, they may think they are better than other people. In fact, when people are prejudiced, they are just demonstrating pride and maybe self-righteousness.

When people start to believe they are better than others, in reality they are beneath those they thought they were better than in the first place!

When people yield to pride, their thoughts are contaminated with how much better they think they are than someone else. People who are prejudiced operate in hate, not love. *"God is love"* (1 John 4:8). So when they operate in pride, their thinking is incorrect, and their thoughts, words, and actions are all wrong. They may even talk badly about certain individuals because they are different in some way.

In fact, pride is all about keeping you bound. Proverbs 4:23 says,

"Keep thy heart with all diligence; for out of it are the issues of life."

When you're thinking and speaking evil, you have tapped into the kingdom of darkness, which allows the enemy and his cohorts access into your life. And all the while, your heart is isolated from the goodness of God.

Remember, if you have a thought about a problem area in your life, and you answer the thought, that thought didn't originate in you.

People yielding to jealousy, envy, or dishonesty can tear someone down with their words.

They say all kinds of things to make them feel better about themselves, but they're hurting on the inside. If someone is lazy, he might make excuses about why he's not getting ahead and someone else is. He might think or talk about how the other person is just lucky.

If your reasoning is based on excuses, you will always wish every day away. You'll want what everyone else has or what they can do, or why they get opportunities you don't. Thoughts will come from the enemy such as, "That's not fair! It's who they know," or, "He must think he's better than me." And all your actions will be based on these thoughts of wanting to isolate and not talk to this person or treating him badly if you do need to talk to him. Then because you are jealous and envious of him, all your words to him or about him have a negative connotation. ALL of this may block or hinder you from doing all you are supposed to do or be.

The enemy is behind negative influences. That is one way he steals, kills, and destroys. There is no positive power of God flowing through negativity.

God's grace is sufficient for you. When you feel weak, His power is strong.

You need to cast down all thoughts that are contrary to the Bible.

In the Old Testament, they fought battles with swords and spears. Sometimes an invading army would come against Israel or there were enemy nations occupying land that was not theirs in the first place, so the children of Israel needed to fight them physically. We, in the New Testament, battle the enemy on his turf, but Jesus has already defeated him for us through His life, death, and resurrection! We get to operate in Jesus' victory with Him, if we are in Him and of Him.

FOR THE FAMILY OF GOD

Many families go on vacation or do something together at least once a year. My question to you is, why didn't you invite me on your last get-together or vacation? The answer is that only the family members get to experience whatever your family does together.

With God, it's the same way. Only the family of God gets to experience everything He is and what He has done. But I have good news!

If you are not a child of God, you can become a child of God, able to experience His goodness and promises every day. The Bible says,

> *"He who calls on the name of the Lord, shall be saved"*
> *(Acts 2:21).*

If you or someone you know does not yet know Jesus personally, I've provided a salvation prayer at the end of the book. Read it and be ready to pray it with anyone in your life who needs to become a child of God so they may enter into eternal life!

Chapter 4
SONS OF GOD

In this chapter, we will study the "sons of God."

Genesis 6:1-4 says,

> "And it came to pass, when men began to multiply on the face of the earth, and daughters were born unto them, that the sons of God saw the daughters of men that they were fair; and they took them wives of all which they chose. And the Lord said, My spirit shall not always strive with man, for that he also is flesh: yet his days shall be an hundred and twenty years. There were giants in the earth in those days; and also after that, when the sons of God came in unto the daughters of men, and they bare children to them, the same became mighty men which were of old, men of renown."

Verse four states that there were giants in the earth in those days, and also after that. It was just stating a fact, not stating a result of the sons of God taking wives from the daughters of men. Their children were of a good reputation. Maybe from the standpoint of the natural man, who was dead unto God, their children were a little more well known. Their blood lines or heritage was a little richer. Remember, Noah's flood will be in one hundred and twenty years. All will die except Noah and his family.

Many years later, the children of Israel saw some giants when they went to spy out the Promise land. Numbers 13:33 says,

> "And there we saw the giants, the sons of Anak, which come of the giants: and we were in our own sight as grasshoppers, and so we were in their sight."

And in David's day, he went face-to-face with Goliath, a giant, the Philistines' champion fighter.

I have seen some pretty big people. They were not the result of fallen angels coming in unto the daughters of men. Let us read through verse 5 of Genesis 6.

It says,

> "And God saw that the wickedness of man was great in the earth, and that every imagination of the thoughts of his heart was only evil continually."

ARE THE FALLEN ANGELS THE SONS OF GOD?

I believe there is a misunderstanding with the term "sons of God." I was taught that fallen angels were the sons of God and they came in to the daughters of men, had children, and the children were giants. Actually, you would have to be taught that to believe that. If that's what you believe, allow me to paint you a more accurate picture about this event.

We need to allow the Bible to interpret the Bible. To begin, who was and is the very first son of God? Correct—the answer is Adam. This answer may not be who you were expecting, but it is true. I can almost hear your mind trying to process this. I think you would like to see in the Bible where it states this.

Alright, in the New Testament, Luke 3:38 says,

> "Which was the son of Enos, which was the son of Seth, which was the son of Adam, which was the son of God."

Now, I am going to split some hairs here. Adam was God's son by creation. This is real deep stuff, but it makes sense.

Genesis 1:26 says,

> "And God [who sits on the throne] said, Let us make man in our image, after our likeness: and let them have dominion."

Genesis 5:1-2 says,

> "This is the book of the generations of Adam. In the day that God [the Word] created man, in the likeness of God [who sits on the throne] made he him; Male and female created he them; and blessed them, and called their name Adam, in the day when they were created".

So, check this out. In Genesis 1:26 God created mankind and communicated with them in heaven. Right then, they were in heaven the way you would be if you had a heavenly experience like John the Revelator. They were spirits and were very alive to God.

The Word of God *"formed man of the dust of the ground, and breathed into his nostrils the breath of life; and man became a living soul." (Genesis 2:7).*

The Word of God was their vehicle from heaven to earth. First of all, I want to show you that Adam operated in the spirit at a level that we try to attain.

THE UNIQUENESS OF ADAM

Did you notice in Genesis 2:19-20 it says that whatever Adam called all the beasts of the field and birds of the air became their name? Did you read here that Adam was a Harvard grad? Yale? Or maybe one of the other Ivy League schools?

Adam was alive unto God, and God was his source. I remember Brother Hagin saying that we are not against education but that people have educated their heads at the expense of their spirits. Adam was created on the sixth day in heaven. On the seventh day, God rested. After the seventh day, Adam was formed and functioning on the earth, naming everything, and using all the grace and ability of God. Did you notice that the first day he was created he could understand God? God told them what to do, and they did it. Once they came into their bodies, they could fulfill God's plan on the earth.

In Genesis 2:21-25, the female side of man was taken out of him.

"So he called her Woman, because she was taken out of man."

Remember, her name is not "Eve" yet. In fact, something I say to people and from which I usually get a reaction is this: Adam and Eve's firstborn child is Cain, according to Genesis 4:1, but Cain is not Adam's first born child.

Because they were in the spirit, names were not as important. Let me explain.

Genesis 5:2 says,

> "Male and female created he them; and blessed them, and called their name Adam, in the day when they were created."

They were alive unto God, and she was known as his wife (see Genesis 2:25 and Genesis 3:8). Also, in Genesis 3:1-2 and 12-13 and in other Scriptures, she is called "*Woman*." Actually Woman was her name. She was her name and her name was her, She was taken out of man.

The name "Eve" wasn't given to her until after they sinned and judgment was given. Genesis 3:20 says,

> "And Adam called his wife's name Eve; because she was the mother of all living."

Now that they were spiritually dead, they had to rely on their intellect, or knowing people by their names. Cain was their first-born after they sinned, but the children born before sin are called "the sons of God." This was God's family—His children that He created and ordained.

They were in the spirit and lived in the spirit. By doing so, they fulfilled all that God told them. Genesis 3:16 says,

> "Unto the woman he said, I will greatly multiply thy sorrow and thy conception; in sorrow thou shalt bring forth children."

There was no pain in childbirth, so they were having children. Up until now the woman wasn't experiencing pain and sorrow in child bearing, but that was about to change. That's what God was telling her about—the consequences because of their choices. God only had to inform them about the changes that had now taken place; He didn't have to mention the things that stayed the same.

Genesis 2:25 says,

> "And they were both naked, the man and his wife, and were not ashamed."

Genesis 3:1 says,

> "Now the serpent was more subtil than any beast of the field which the Lord God had made. And he said unto the woman, Yea, hath God said, Ye shall not eat of every tree of the garden?"

In between them cleaving together and the serpent coming on the scene was over one hundred years. During this time, they were having children, and their children were having children. Their children's children were having children, and so on, and so forth.

MY VISION

From here we need understanding. The Lord gave me a vision. Now, I don't want to tell you the whole vision, but I was standing behind a pulpit when Jesus suddenly appeared on my left side. And I asked Him, "Would you like to speak?"

When he was standing at my left side, I didn't look at Him intently, but I knew it was Him in my heart. He didn't have His name on His shirt, or a button that said, "I'm the Master," or, "Savior," but, in my spirit, I knew. It wasn't based on my intellect, because I had never seen Him before. In my spirit I just knew.

BRINGING IT ALL TOGETHER

Know that man lived and operated in the spirit at a level where they were both naked, the man and his wife, and were not ashamed (see Genesis 2:25). They didn't operate through their intellects, because that would be limited. They operated through their spirits, which was almost limitless.

They were hooked up to the unlimited God. In fact, they operated at the same level that Jesus did—until they sinned.

They had one advantage over Jesus; they didn't have to deal with the devil and his bunch, but Jesus did. Remember that man had the Word of God. The Word of God was walking in the garden in the cool of the day, looking for man (Genesis 3:8).

Let's look more at the sons of God with the perfect bloodline. Recapping, the sons of God were Adam and the woman, all the children born from them, and their grandchildren, and all the children born before sin or through people who hadn't sinned. They were still alive unto God as sons of God. The sons of God married the daughters of God. They had children of God. This is the family of God or the people of God.

They were not covenant people, but blood-created blood people.

The sons of man, or the daughters of man, were Adam and Eve and all the children born from them after they sinned and were dead spiritually. Sons of man also referred to the intermixing from the two camps—the sons of God, or sons of men, and daughters of God, or daughters of men.

So, there was a people who were spiritually alive-the sons of God. But there was also a people who were spiritually dead, whose god (the prince of this world, Satan) was spiritually dead. These spiritually dead people have to operate through their intellect with all the forces of death working for them.

You need to understand about the sons of God and the daughters of men: they didn't have 2 Corinthians 6:14, which says,

> "Be ye not unequally yoked together with unbelievers: for what fellowship hath righteousness with unrighteousness? and what communion hath light with darkness?"

The enemy's goal was to corrupt, or pervert, the sons of God and their bloodline—totally erasing God's family from the earth. The less of God, or the fewer people of God, the easier it is for the enemy to rule and reign.

In Job, we have a couple of situations with the sons of God, let's look at them together.

JOB AND THE SONS OF GOD

God talked very highly of Job. He is called God's servant (see Job 1:8). I believe Job was a son of God as I explained it above, and it classifies him in a day when the sons of God came to present themselves. You should read the book of Job for insight.

Job 1:6 says, *"Now there was a day when the sons of God came to present themselves before the Lord, and Satan came also among them."*

Job 2:1 says,

"Again there was a day when the sons of God came to present themselves before the Lord, and Satan came also among them to present himself before the Lord."

Based on Job, every so often the sons of God presented themselves before the Lord. It was almost like a believers meeting or a family reunion. Just a side note: anywhere Satan and his cohorts can go, they will go. They are persistent, looking for opportunities that we give them.

WHO GOD BLESSED AND EMPOWERED

I want to say this before we go any further. Genesis 1:28 tells us about Adam and his wife, *"And God blessed them, and God said unto them, Be fruitful, and multiply, and replenish the earth, and subdue it: and have dominion over the fish of the sea, over the fowl of the air, and over every living thing that moves upon the earth."* This is who God blessed to replenish the earth and to be fruitful and to multiply after their kind. The ability, the truth, and the power are in the creatures of this earth, not the angelic host.

I think we imagine that the devil has more power than he really has. The law of Genesis is that everything would produce after its kind.

God the Creator created life-bearing creatures to produce after their kind and humans to produce after their kind. You can't crossbreed anything out of its family.

In the Gospel of John 4:24 we read,

> "God is a Spirit: and they that worship him must worship him in spirit and in truth."

God legally can't crossbreed out of his family. Now, God created every living thing, but man was created after God's likeness and in His image with dominion (see Genesis 1:26-27).

Also, 1 Thessalonians 5:23 says,

> "And the very God of peace sanctify you wholly; and I pray God your whole spirit and soul and body be preserved blameless unto the coming of our Lord Jesus Christ."

So, from this and other Scriptures we covered earlier, we know man is a spirit, like God.

Remember, God formed a body out of the dust of the ground, which He created. The body was formed in His image and after His likeness (see Genesis 2:7). Now, we will never be deity, or absolute, or all knowing, or everywhere at once, but our Father is. God the Creator, who is all-powerful, wanted a natural family with free will on the earth. God also doesn't just want children—He wants children who want Him.

Now, He needs to redeem the old family and start a new one. I heard a story one day of a dad and his son shopping. The son was asking his dad for this and that, and the dad was saying "no" to everything. And, finally, the son blurted out, "I didn't ask to be born." And the dad said, "If you had, the answer would have been NO." In the natural realm, we don't have any say in who our father is, but in the spiritual realm, we do.

BABIES AND FATHERHOOD

One day, back in the 80's, I was driving my truck in western Oklahoma, and the Lord spoke to me. It sounded like an audible voice. It probably wasn't, but it sounded like it was. He said, "You know the physical way that a baby gets into its mother's womb. How does the spirit get in there?"

So I thought, "Well, does He just say, 'Spirit, be'?" I didn't know, so I prayed, "Lord, you said in Matthew 7:7-8,

> 'Ask, and it shall be given you; seek, and ye shall find; knock, and it shall be opened unto you: For every one that asketh receiveth; and he that seeketh findeth; and to him that knocketh it shall be opened.'

So, I'm asking you, 'How does the spirit get in there?' And, I thank you for the answer in your holy name."

So, I prayed that day and the next day. And on the third day, I pressed in a little more, and went through Matthew 7:7-8 again. A little bit later that day, the Lord said, "The life of the seed and the life of the egg is the spirit."

I said, "Oh, so we are spirit-reproducing people." A few seconds later I said, "Why did you ask me that question?"

He said, "So I could answer it."

I said, "You just do that any time you want to!"

The Word of God was not the Son of God until the Word was made flesh and dwelt among us (John 1:14). God, who sits on the throne, became His Father, but not until He fathered Him. There are lots of names that represent Him, but until He fathered Jesus, He could not be called His Father. God fathered Adam through creation. He fathered Jesus through the angel speaking to Mary and she received the Word by faith. Let's look at when God became the father of Jesus.

Luke 1:27-37 says,

> *"To a virgin espoused to a man whose name was Joseph, of the house of David; and the virgin's name was Mary. And the angel came in unto her, and said, Hail, thou that art highly favoured, the Lord is with thee: blessed art thou among women. And when she saw him, she was troubled at his saying, and cast in her mind what manner of salutation this should be.*
>
> *And the angel said unto her, Fear not, Mary: for thou hast found favour with God. And, behold, thou shalt conceive in thy womb, and bring forth a son, and shalt call his name Jesus. He shall be great, and shall be called the Son of the Highest: and the Lord God shall give unto him the throne of his father David:*
>
> *And he shall reign over the house of Jacob for ever; and of his kingdom there shall be no end. Then said Mary unto the angel, How shall this be, seeing I know not a man? And the angel answered and said unto her, The Holy Ghost shall come upon thee, and the power of the Highest shall overshadow thee: therefore also that holy thing which shall be born of thee shall be called the Son of God.*
>
> *And, behold, thy cousin Elisabeth, she hath also conceived a son in her old age: and this is the sixth month with her, who was called barren. For with God nothing shall be impossible."*

Naturally speaking, when the seed of a man unites with the egg of a woman, we call that "conception". With God, it's a little different. God is a spirit, and God operates by faith. Jesus said in a parable in Luke 8:11, *"...The seed is the word of God."* You could also say that the Word of God is the seed. When God sowed the word through his angel, all that was left was conception. Let us proceed to verse 38. It says, *"And Mary said, Behold the handmaid of the Lord; be it unto me according to thy word. And the angel departed from her."*

By faith, she received the Word. Conception was fulfilled. She was now pregnant by the Word of God and with the Word of God. Because God fathered this Child, He was now known as God the Father. Remember that God named His Son Jesus (see Luke 1:31).

Actually, God is now His Father. Do you want to know how He becomes your Father?

See, in natural conception, it takes the seed of a man and the egg of a woman. But then, you don't have a bunch of seed and a bunch of egg. No, you have something altogether different. You have a baby. God is a Spirit, and God sent His Spirit. So, when people receive Jesus as their Lord and Savior, the Spirit of Truth comes into their spirit.

Now, your spirit is dead spiritually—separated from God. And, the Spirit of Truth is life. When He comes into you, you become something different also. In 2 Corinthians 5:17 Paul says,

> "Therefore if any man be in Christ, he is a new creature: old things are passed away; behold, all things are become new."

Now, when you receive Jesus as your Lord and Savior, you're not a dead spirit and a spirit of life together, just like a baby isn't simply a collection of seed and egg—you are a new creature in Christ. Spiritually, you have been reborn by God. You have become something altogether different. You are now a new creature in Christ. So, he is now your Father. He just fathered you spiritually. Now, you are His son or daughter in Christ.

That's why Jesus said in John 3:6,

> "That which is born of the flesh is flesh; and that which is born of the Spirit is spirit. "

In 1 Peter 1:23 it says,

> "Being born again, not of corruptible seed, but of incorruptible, by the word of God, which liveth and abideth for ever."

We read in 1 Corinthians 15:45,

> "And so it is written, The first man Adam was made a living soul; the last Adam was made a quickening spirit."

All the people who have been born again are the sons of God. We are in the family of God on the earth again, and we operate in the Kingdom of God. He is not just our Father but our Daddy.

Jesus referred to his Father in Mark 14:36 which says,

> "And he said, Abba, Father, all things are possible unto thee; take away this cup from me: nevertheless not what I will, but what thou wilt."

And in Romans 8:15 it says,

> "For ye have not received the spirit of bondage again to fear; but ye have received the Spirit of adoption, whereby we cry, Abba, Father."

Galatians 4:6 says,

> "And because ye are sons, God hath sent forth the Spirit of his Son into your hearts, crying, Abba, Father."

God doesn't just want to father you; He wants an intimate relationship with you every day.

Like I said, the devil was out to rid the earth of God's family, but because of what Jesus did in His life, death, burial, and resurrection, God's ultimate act of love—paying the price for sin—was a cost greater than what man could pay.

He did it to get His family back.

Just think, we are not born into His family by chance. We choose. It's our decision as to whether we are born again into His family. He lets us choose. If you read Acts 2:41, you read that three thousand souls were added to the number of those who believed. So there were added about three thousand new children in one day. Also Acts 4:4 says that five thousand were added that day. God was replenishing the earth with His family.

God's family is growing on the earth. And, as we tell the Good News to others, His family gets larger.

I hope this exploration of the words "sons of God" has answered some questions for you. One we didn't cover but has been used to harass Christians for years is, "Where did Cain get his wife?" I feel like we answered this as well, as a free bonus!

Genesis 4:16-17 says that Cain's wife would have been from the family of the sons of God.

Genesis 4:14 says,

> "Behold, thou hast driven me out this day from the face of the earth; and from thy face shall I be hid; and I shall be a fugitive and a vagabond in the earth; and it shall come to pass, that every one that findeth me shall slay me."

After God cursed Cain, the only people alive are Adam, Eve, Cain, and the sons of God. Cain was very concerned that anyone who finds him would kill him.

Genesis 4:15 says,

> "And the Lord said unto him, Therefore whosoever slayeth Cain, vengeance shall be taken on him sevenfold. And the Lord set a mark upon Cain, lest any finding him should kill him."

So, the sons of God were functioning at a higher spiritual level than just plain, ordinary intellect, or according to their five physical senses. So Cain did have a true concern.

One thing I remember about Kenneth E. Hagin is that he would share about a vision that had happened forty years earlier. He was in the Spirit, and he would say that spiritual things don't get old. It would seem to him as if it had happened last Saturday night.

Chapter 5
THE SERPENT AND OTHER ANIMALS OF THE KINGDOMS

When we look at the earliest records of life, the prophet Jeremiah paints a very accurate picture. In Jeremiah 4:23-28 we see the condition of the earth, as the judgment of God is being executed. We gain some insight in Jeremiah 4:25 where the prophet wrote,

> "I beheld, and, lo, there was no man, and all the birds of the heaven were fled."

First of all, the physical heaven wasn't created or made yet. So this was referring to the spiritual heaven, where God who sits on the throne is, or another part of heaven.

Let's examine this other part of heaven for a moment. The Apostle Paul talked about being caught up to the third heaven in 2 Corinthians 12:2-4:

> "I knew a man in Christ above fourteen years ago, (whether in the body, I cannot tell; or whether out of the body, I cannot tell: God knoweth;) such an one caught up to the third heaven. And I knew such a man, (whether in the body, or out of the body, I cannot tell: God knoweth;) How that he was caught up into paradise, and heard unspeakable words, which it is not lawful for a man to utter."

He called the third heaven paradise. This is the place where Jesus would have congregated with the living on the other side. Ephesians 4:8 says,

> "Wherefore he saith, When he ascended up on high, he led captivity captive, and gave gifts unto men."

Remember what Jesus said to one of the thieves while they were hanging on the cross? *"And Jesus said unto him, Verily I say unto thee, Today shalt thou be with me in paradise."* (Luke 23:43).

So, to what exact part of heaven did all the birds of heaven flee? It's uncertain, but there must have been a great ruckus in heaven when this event of judgment was occurring. The "birds of heaven" was Jeremiah's perspective, what he saw. We never want to add or take away from Scripture, and I don't know if we can say for certain, but could the cities that Jeremiah saw have been from the kingdom of darkness' creatures?

Also, just because the Bible uses the word "city" doesn't mean it is what we consider a physical city to look like.

Also notice, there was no man at this point. The Apostle Paul writes in 1 Corinthians 15:45,

> "And so it is written, The first man Adam was a living soul; the last Adam was made a quickening spirit."

He said the "first man," not the first man after this or that. Adam was created in the image of God and after His likeness (see Genesis 1:26-27). Genesis 5:1-2 says,

> "This is the book of the generations of Adam. In the day that God [the Word] created man, in the likeness of God [who sits on the throne] made he him. Male and female created he them; and blessed them, and called their name Adam, in the day when they were created."

Notice the word "them" and "their," plural, meaning both of them. Both spirits, male and female, are called Adam, and were created on the sixth day. Sometime after, Adam was formed of the dust of the ground on the physical earth. This was to be his earthly tabernacle that he would possess. Therefore, Adam is a spirit, which is an eternal being, and Adam is physical, which is an earthly being.

Genesis 2:19-20 describes the Lord forming the animals and Adam naming them. But there was no comparable helper for Adam. Look at Genesis 2:21-23:

> "And the Lord God caused a deep sleep to fall upon Adam, and he slept: and he took one of his ribs, and he closed up the flesh instead theoreof; And the rib, which the Lord God had taken from the man, made he a woman, and brought her unto the man. And Adam said, This is now bone of my bones, and flesh of my flesh: she shall be called Woman, because she was taken out of Man."

Let me reiterate verse 23: "...*she shall be called Woman, because she was taken out of Man.*"

I believe the name Adam and Woman has a stronger, more important meaning than how we use it today. God created them, communicated with them, and called their name Adam in the day they were created. Then a body was formed for them of the dust of the ground on the earth. So they were two spirits, and the spirit of life, or breath of life, in one body. Don't forget, this is the image and the likeness of God.

If you have been born again, the Spirit of Truth came inside your dead spirit and you became a new creature in Christ, so that is two different spirits, one spiritually dead and another spiritually alive—although related by the Spirit of life—becoming one spirit in one physical body.

We read in 1 Corinthians 12:13:

> *"For by one Spirit are we all baptized into one body, whether we be Jews or Gentiles, whether we be bond or free; and have been all made to drink into one Spirit."*

We are the Body of Christ and members in particular. Christ means "Anointed One," and we know the Anointed One is God's [who sits on the throne] Son, His only begotten Son, Jesus. We are all physically alive because of the breath of life—everyone is included. But to become spiritually alive, as we become when we decide to receive Jesus as our Lord and Savior—only God can do that. Our spirit becomes one with the Spirit of Truth. We become a new creature in Christ. We are now a son of God, adopted into the family of God. We are now in fellowship and communion with God [who sits on the throne]. And everything He is, we have access to; and everything He is, is good.

This is just a side thought, but this is related: When a husband and wife come together and the wife is impregnated, the husband has played his part in the conception of the baby. The baby that is now growing and developing in the womb is a part of the wife. She has a spiritual, emotional, and physical connection to this baby.

God took the rib out of man, and the female side out of man, and closed up the flesh. (He called her woman because she was taken out of man, right?)

She was on the inside of him, and a part of him, his rib, went in to making her physically. That keeps them as one. Some of the same structure, of the dust formation, which came alive with the breath of life, was used in building the woman. They are one flesh (see Genesis 2:24). So two different events, but related by God.

ANGELS AND ANIMALS

According to Jeremiah, there was an animal kingdom in the midst at the judgment event, at least in heaven. Remember, in Genesis 1:20 God created life in the waters and in the air. So in what we call creation (or the re-creation), on the fifth day God created some of the animals, but birds in particular. The bird kingdom was among the first life-bearing animals created on the fifth day. But in Jeremiah 4:25 we see all the birds of the heavens had fled.

Remember, there would have been a process to how God created and made creatures. When you look at some of the angels or creatures in heaven, some of them have wings. Also, on the sixth day He created more animals, and mankind in His image and after His likeness. Don't forget, there was not time as we know it—this was in everlasting.

If you look at all the accounts of the heavenly host, you see most of them with the appearance of something from the animal kingdom, at least as we know it. In heaven they are called "creatures." They are different levels of angels, made for different tasks.

In Ezekiel 10:8,14 we read,

"And there appeared in the cherubims the form of a man's hand under their wings... And every one had four faces: the first face was the face of a cherub, and the second face was the face of a man, and the third face was the face of a lion, and the fourth face of an eagle."

So there are some of the angelic host with certain similar features as a man and others with features that resemble animals.

If you would have had this heavenly account by an angel, before man was created and made, the angel would have said, "It resembles a hand like God's hand under their wings."

And in 10:14, he would have stated that the second face resembles the face of God. Ezekiel spoke from his perspective, and so would we. Man was created in God's image and after His likeness, with dominion. God created angels with a purpose and for a purpose. Speaking of angels, the writer of Hebrews 1:14 tells us, *"Are they not all ministering spirits, sent forth to minister for them who shall be heirs of salvation?"*

Getting back to Genesis, I told you when the Word of God was creating animals, that God, who sits on the throne, on five different occasions said, "after his kind," implying ownership, or like the ones he has already made. Remember, everything that was created and made in heaven and on earth, visible and invisible, was created and made by the person of the Trinity whose name is called the Word of God.

Lucifer was an angel of light, full of wisdom and perfect in beauty, till iniquity was found in him (see Ezekiel 28:12-15). He is no longer Lucifer; he's now the devil or Satan. After he fell from his position in heaven, he deceived one third of the angels, and they were cast to the earth. Remember what Jesus said in Luke 10:18: *"I beheld Satan as lightning fall from heaven."*

Jude 1:6 tells us,

> *"And the angels which kept not their first estate, but left their own habitation, he hath reserved in everlasting chains under darkness unto the judgment of the great day."*

Continue reading Jude 1:13:

> *"Raging waves of the sea, foaming out their own shame; wandering stars, to whom is reserved the blackness of darkness for ever."*

So now read again Genesis 1:2:

> "And the earth was without form, and void; and darkness was upon the face of the deep. And the Spirit of God moved upon the face of the waters."

Now, Satan is an angel of darkness. In fact, he is the king of that domain—the kingdom of spiritual darkness.

Genesis 3:1 tells us that the serpent was more subtle than any other animal. It is implying the serpent is on a different level than the beast of the fields, but not saying he is more subtle than any beast of heaven, just the natural beast. Some people say that the devil used the body of a snake to talk to the woman. I don't believe that. I believe the devil spoke to the woman the same way he speaks to you and me today.

Revelation 12:9 tells us,

> "And the great dragon was cast out, that old serpent, called the Devil, and Satan, which deceiveth the whole world: he was cast out into the earth, and his angels were cast out with him."

If you think about it, snakes don't walk, they slither. Notice in Job 1:7 it says,

> "And the Lord said unto Satan, Whence comest thou? Then Satan answered the Lord, and said, From going to and fro in the earth, and from walking up and down in it."

I believe the dragon or the serpent would be, in our vernacular, something like a lizard or something like an alligator—something of that family design, walking on his belly.

THE CURSE

In Genesis 3:14 we read,

> "And the Lord God said unto the serpent, because thou hast done this, thou art cursed above all cattle, and above every beast of the field; upon thy belly shall thou go, and dust shalt thou eat all the days of thy life."

The devil is an angel, but did you notice in his judgment by the Word of God that the comparisons were to that of the earthly animal kingdom? I believe the dust that he shall eat is spiritual dust, not natural, physical dust. Also, when the serpent came on the scene in Genesis 3:1 it says,

> "Now the serpent was more subtil than any beast of the field which the Lord God had made."

He is stating here that the serpent is more cunning than any other animal of the field on earth, but not implying that he is more cunning than any beast of heaven. So are you seeing the animal kingdoms?

ANGELS

There are different levels of angels. God, who created everything, created them with different responsibilities and tasks. Man was created in His image and after His likeness. God created animals, creatures, beasts, and creeping things in heaven and on earth. The devil has greater abilities than the earthly animals because he's not earthly but a spiritual being or creature. He can communicate in your language; animals cannot. He can whisper in your thought process, and you can think about what you hear him say.

In our mind when we picture the devil, he probably looks like a man—maybe with two horns coming out of the top of his head, also maybe the color red, with a tail, and a pitchfork in his hand. At least, that's what most Halloween costumes make him out to look like. Well, actually, the devil does have a tail. Revelation 12:4 *"And his tail drew the third part of the stars of heaven…"*

I think one reason the devil is so hateful toward us and jealous and envious of us is because we were created in the image of God and after His likeness. The devil and all his cohorts are animalistic creatures. This is one reason the devil is so hateful toward us and jealous and envious of us. God created man in His own image after His likeness and gave him dominion over all the animal kingdom and over all the earth, which includes the entire physical planet and the inhabitants of the planet.

Here is some food for thought: People I greatly respect have operated in the spiritual gift of the discerning of spirits. And when they saw a demon, in every case that I heard, they said it looked like a little imp or a little monkey. They were creatures that resemble our physical animals, causing havoc with man. Also, talking about evil spirits, Jesus said in Luke 10:19,

> *"Behold, I give unto you power to tread on serpents and scorpions, and over all the power of the enemy: and nothing shall by any means hurt you."*

These are not physical serpents and scorpions but spiritual serpents and scorpions. Jesus was probably referring to what they look like in the spirit realm. Revelation 16:13 shows us,

> *"And I saw three unclean spirits like frogs come out of the mouth of the dragon, and out of the mouth of the beast, and out of the mouth of the false prophet."*

Also note in the beginning of verse 14 it says,

> *"For they are spirits of devils…"*

We don't need to know what they look like; we have authority over them no matter what size, shape, color, or ability.

They have all been stripped of power and brought to nothing, as far as heaven and earth and the believer is concerned.

ANGELS THAT LIVE IN THE SEA

I would like to touch on one more scripture concerning fallen angels. Revelation 20:13 says,

> "And the sea gave up the dead which were in it; and death and hell delivered up the dead which were in them: and they were judged every man according to their works."

I asked someone what did that mean, that the sea gave up the dead which was in it? They said they thought it was the people who died in the sea.

When a person's spirit and soul departs from his earthly body, it travels up to heaven if that person is born again through faith in Jesus Christ. If a person is not born again through faith in Jesus Christ, then that person's spirit departs down to hell and waits on his judgment. Don't forget, spiritual death is being separated from God, being without God.

Some of the fallen angels are held captive in the spiritual sea, which seemingly is located in our physical sea. The sea is the location where the waters are congregated, the physical structure, or bowl, that holds the water. Habakkuk 2:14 says,

> "For the earth shall be filled with the knowledge of the glory of the Lord, as the waters cover the sea."

Also Isaiah 11:9 says,

> "They shall not hurt nor destroy in all my holy mountain: for the earth shall be full of the knowledge of the Lord, as the waters cover the sea."

There are fallen angels, with the appearance of animals because they are creatures, that are held captive in the spiritual sea.

Also in Revelation 9:14,

"Saying to the sixth angel which had a trumpet, Loose the four angels which are bound in the great river Euphrates."

Now I know that God speaks in symbols and in mysteries, but God in his infinite wisdom also speaks from what things look like in the spiritual realm. And don't forget spiritual laws and physical laws are totally different. For instance, Revelation 13:1-2 says,

"And I stood upon the sand of the sea, and I saw a beast rise up out of the sea, having seven heads and ten horns, and upon his horns ten crowns, and upon his ten heads the name of blasphemy. And the beast which I saw was like unto a leopard, and his feet were as the feet of a bear, and his mouth as the mouth of a lion: and the dragon gave him his power, and his seat, and great authority."

This beast, naturally speaking, is not a sea creature. He is a fallen angel. He is an angelic spirit, separated from God. He is spiritually dead, and awaiting judgment and the lake of fire. This is the second death.

Now check this out in Isaiah 27:1:

"In that day the Lord with his sore and great and strong sword shall punish leviathan the piercing serpent, even leviathan that crooked serpent; and he shall slay the dragon that is in the sea."

So God is just telling us about events that will happen. I believe the devil and his cohorts don't have any power over the children of God, unless we give it to them through sin, or just being lazy and complacent. Father forgive us. As these different creatures are loosed they can affect their domain.

One more reference to creatures of light and of darkness is found in Revelation 5:13,

> "And every creature which is in heaven, and on the earth, and under the earth, and such as are in the sea, and all that are in them, heard I saying, Blessing, and honour, and glory, and power, be unto him that sitteth upon the throne, and unto the Lamb for ever and ever."

THE SERPENT AND THE WORD OF GOD

The serpent, when speaking to the woman, said in Genesis 3:5:

> "For God doth know that in the day ye eat thereof, then your eyes shall be opened, and ye shall be as gods knowing good and evil."

In all the conversations between God and man, God never once said that her eyes would be opened. So how did the serpent or the devil know this? Well, I'm glad you asked.

When Lucifer sinned in his heart, his eyes were opened, as he traveled as lightning out of heaven to the earth, along with the angels he deceived.

The word "knowing" as we see in Genesis 3:5 deceivingly means you will not function through your spirit, but because of your disobedience, you will now function through your soul or your five physical senses. This was man's spiritual death.

Everything about God is good, and He is Spirit. Man has lost the ability to tap into the spiritual realm, where God's kingdom domain is alive and active.

The serpent said in Genesis 3:5 that if they ate, *"Ye shall be as gods, knowing good and evil."*

And then in Genesis 3:22 it says,

> "And the Lord God said, Behold, the man is become **as one of us**, to know good and evil."

My question to you is, which one did they become like? They became like one of them.

Which one? Job 1:6-7:

> "Now there was a day when the sons of God came to present themselves before the Lord, and Satan came also among them. And the Lord said unto Satan, whence comest thou? Then Satan answered the Lord, From going to and fro in the earth, and from walking up and down in it."

The answer is that the Word of God entered into a relationship with the devil by default. When the devil got kicked out of heaven, there was only one other place to go, the earth.

I had a pastor who lived next door to a vacant house. When the new owners moved in next door to him, they brought their two barking dogs. My pastor entered into a relationship with the family, and the two barking dogs, by default.

Remember in Matthew 19:16-17 when the man came to Jesus and said,

> "And, behold, one came and said unto him, Good Master, what good thing shall I do, that I may have eternal life? And he said unto him, Why callest thou me good? there is none good but one, that is, God: but if thou wilt enter into life, keep the commandments."

God is good; the devil is evil. They already knew the one who is good. The problem is, you can't serve two masters. And in their disobedience, they were deceived—but they chose not the God of the Spirit who created, but the god of the physical realm, who was a created creature and who, according to his own words, is evil.

APPLYING TO YOUR LIFE

Let's look at the word "knowing." In Genesis 3:5, knowing good and evil has with it a commitment and relationship attached to it. God's desire was for His family to be so hooked up and committed to Him in the spirit that if God breathed out, spirit would come out of our mouths.

We look like Him. We should act like Him. That's why Jesus came and died for mankind, so that we could be born again with the Spirit of Truth, or life and nature of God, living on the inside of us and flowing through us—God's DNA if you will. We have the written Word of God, so we can get to know God our Abba Father, Jesus our Savior, and the Holy Spirit intimately. God's desire is an intimate relationship with us individually.

The one thing that hinders our relationship is sin. That is why God doesn't want us to sin. Sin gives the devil an inroad, a damaging and serious encroachment into our life.

Let's take jealousy for example. Suppose you are jealous of a person; then you won't act in love towards that person. Your thoughts will be that of envy, making excuses for your behavior, maybe murmuring and complaining, or even lying. When you speak out of your jealousy, it will never be the truth.

Look at James 3:16:

> *"For where envy and strife is, there is confusion and every evil work."*

The children of Israel, when they were in the wilderness, hardened their hearts, not mixing what God said with faith. It says they tested God (see Hebrews 3:9).

A person operating in jealousy is not walking in love, *"for God is love"* (1 John 4:9).

You're also not walking in faith, for *"without faith it is impossible to please God"* (Hebrews 11:6). You're walking with a hardened heart toward God and that person. The Bible says faith works by love.

Also, the Father seeks those who will worship Him in spirit and in truth. When your heart is troubled because of unresolved sin, you can't enter into worship. If you're not walking by faith in God, and you're not walking in the love of God, I can guarantee you're not walking in the peace of God and you're not pleasing God.

If every step you take in your walk with the Lord, you are testing Him, then He has no pleasure in you, then you can't worship Him in spirit and in truth.

Who then do you look like? That's why the Bible says to give no place to the devil. He is not out for your best but he's out for your worst. Allow the Word of God to dwell in you richly, and keep Him first place in your life. Then you shall know the truth, and the truth shall set you free.

SALVATION PRAYER

Romans 10:9-10 says,

> *"That if thou shalt confess with thy mouth the Lord Jesus, and shalt believe in thine heart that God hath raised him from the dead, thou shalt be saved. For with the heart man believeth unto righteousness; and with the mouth confession is made unto salvation."*

The importance of this prayer is that you mean what you pray with all your heart.

If so, pray aloud,

"Heavenly Father, in the name of Jesus, I ask you to forgive me of my sins.

In your Word in John 1:12 it says, *"But as many as received him, to them gave he power to become the sons of God, even to them that believe on his name."* So I receive Jesus, your Son, as my Savior.

I believe that you raised Him from the dead, and I give Jesus the lordship of my life. Lord Jesus, use my life for your glory, and give me the power to change my life, that I may live and know you, the Father, and the Holy Spirit more intimately every day of my life. Amen."

Now you are a child of God, and God is now your Father! Angels are rejoicing in heaven.

Luke 15:10 says,

> *"Likewise, I say unto you, there is joy in the presence of the angels of God over one sinner that repenteth."*

Ephesians 2:8-9 tells us,

> *"For by grace are you saved through faith; and that not of yourselves: it is the gift of God: Not of works, lest any man should boast."*

WELCOME TO THE FAMILY OF GOD!

NOTES

NOTES